FOOTBALL   Designing the Beautiful Game

edited by Eleanor Watson
and James Bird

the DESIGN MUSEUM

Director's Foreword
Tim Marlow

The origins of football are ancient. The great civilisations of China, Egypt, Greece and Mexico all had games that involved the kicking of a ball, but the roots of modern football were in Britain, from medieval mob games to the codifiers of Victorian England (and Scotland) who established a set of rules that have been constantly challenged but broadly adhered to for the past 150 years. This is not in any way to claim cultural ownership of the game along nationalistic lines, but rather to highlight the breadth of its origins and its universal resonance as well as underscoring just how intense the development of the world's most popular sport has been.

There are numerous ways of viewing the rapid rise of football as a global phenomenon over the last century and a half – from the amateur to the professional; from an impromptu playground sport to a mass mediated international spectacle – but perhaps the most interesting if underplayed is to explore it through the lens of design. In everything from the ball itself to the boots and kit the players wear, from the pitches and stadiums where the game is played to the tournaments and television coverage and much more besides, there is a design story.

This book is published to accompany the first major exhibition devoted to design and football, to the work of architects, engineers, inventors, designers and indeed fans who have shaped the game. There are some major creative players included, not least Archibald Leitch, Jacques Herzog, Eduardo Souto de Moura, Martine Rose and Paul Barnes, but unlike the cult of the superstar footballer that is so central to the modern game, most of the designers of what have become among the most prominent objects across the globe are still largely anonymous. We seek to redress that imbalance to some extent, but more broadly our aim is to explore and celebrate the impact of design on what the legendary Brazilian Pelé called the 'beautiful game' – which it certainly was when he played it – but also to acknowledge the fundamental tension between idealism and pragmatism which both football and design are constantly negotiating and from which so much ingenuity results.

As with the game itself, the mounting of this exhibition has relied on teamwork. I would like to thank our content partners, the National Football Museum, who have been so generous in sharing numerous treasures from their collection, as well as their expertise. I would also like to thank Snap and the Italian Trade Agency for their support.

Introduction
James Bird and Eleanor Watson

'Football is a sport made from spontaneity and discernment, luxury and freedom.'
– Sócrates

Football is the world's most popular sport. It is estimated that more than half the Earth's population – some 3.5 billion people – watched part of the FIFA World Cup in 2018, while 265 million regularly play the game. It occupies a unique position in our cultural landscape, shaping people's timetables, the way they dress, and how they relate to their families, their communities and their cities. Once every four years, football even affects the way we think about national identity. It defines – and designs – the way many of us live.

Yet while football is part of the everyday, it is also highly manufactured. It is both a simple game and a complex industry, drawing on a vast pool of specialists to push the sport to its technical and emotional limits. This catalogue, and the exhibition it accompanies, is an exploration of the people and processes that have made football what it is today. From the early days of amateur sport through to the present level of professionalisation and intense mediatisation, it brings to light the architects, engineers, inventors, designers and fans who have shaped football, as both a sport and a spectacle. It is the design story behind a global phenomenon.

Anyone can play football at little cost, which allows talent and creativity to flourish in incredibly diverse settings. Unlike sports such as tennis, golf or gymnastics, it doesn't depend on expensive equipment and it can be played almost anywhere. The only essential requirement is a ball, and even this can be fashioned from any number of humble materials. This accessibility is often pointed to as the reason for the game's immense popularity.

As with all professional sports, however, football is forever searching for a competitive edge. From lightweight boots that offer greater freedom of movement, and more aerodynamic balls, to shock-absorbent pitches and restorative exercise routines, the football industry is continually devising new tools to enable teams to play longer, faster and more consistently. The development of these tools presents a concise history of football's professionalisation, illustrating the ever-increasing resources that are dedicated to producing elite athletes.

A wonderful example of this comes in the form of the humble football stud. Initially simple leather discs nailed on to the soles of boots, studs gained an almost mythical status after the 1954 FIFA World Cup final. As the story goes, West Germany had a two-goal deficit to the tournament's favourites, Hungary, when Adi Dassler (the founder of adidas) had the ingenious idea of fitting the German team's boots with longer studs. These were better suited to the rain-soaked pitch, and saw the German side come back to win 3-2, an event known for evermore as the 'Miracle of Bern'.

The West German team wearing the 'Miracle of Bern' boots, 1954

Technical ingenuity trumped raw talent, and the role of design in the pursuit of marginal gains has remained uncontested ever since. Today complex arrangements of multidirectional oval studs are the norm, with sports brands pouring huge resources into developing specialist materials and manufacturing methods to allow for greater grip and control. Some of these designs are almost too effective, though, and the abrupt stopping and starting that they allow puts considerable strain on the player's body. Designers are finding increasingly subtle ways to circumvent these physical limits, with wholly personalised designs set to become standard practice in the future.

Introduction

Footballers are very much creatures of habit, and getting the mind and body to a state where both can perform at the highest level requires things to be … just right. The innovation of performance brands means that equipment across the board is constantly evolving, but there are some things that stay the same. From elite professionals to Sunday League amateurs through to post-work five-a-side matches in AstroTurf complexes across the globe, tape, with its myriad uses, has been a pre-match changing-room saviour that is still passed down from generation to generation. Tape might be used to cover an earring, so the referee doesn't spot a player wearing it ten minutes into a game and make them take time off the pitch to remove it. Or it might be used to wrap around an ankle at the base of a shinpad to ensure the pad doesn't fall down and disrupt the player's ability to control the ball. Of course, shinpads have evolved to include ankle guards, and socks are constructed so they no longer fall down, but still the sound of the humble tape being taken out of a sports bag, unwound and wrapped around various parts of the body remains present around the world.

Football is a game that people cling on to through their memories, and over the years, pieces of performance design have become so synonymous with a specific player or moment that football fans could identify them just by looking at an object. Show a football fan an adidas Jabulani, the official ball for the 2010 FIFA World Cup, and they are likely to start shouting 'Tshabalalaaa!' after the South African player Siphiwe Tshabalala, who scored the incredible opening goal of the tournament for the host nation. A pair of orange-shaded sports glasses could only ever represent Dutch footballer and Champions League winner Edgar Davids. And of course, inflatable plastic unicorns belong to the recent England squads, specifically Bukayo Saka and the 'glorious purpose' Ian Wright anointed him with. Football performance pieces, even the most revolution-ary ones in terms of design, are made iconic by the moments that are created in them.

In organised games of football, it is important to be able to distinguish one set of players from another. This is as vital for those on the pitch as for spectators following developments from a distance. In its simplest

One use of tape on the football pitch

form, this need for identification might lead, for example, to one team being dressed in blue and the other in red. But what began as a practical solution has evolved into an incredibly rich and diverse world of football graphics, with the team kit – its colours and crest – acting as a foundation. The production and dissemination of football graphics has become a seemingly all-pervasive global network, with football kits creating unlikely links across the world. In the words of Malian-French photographer Émile-Samory Fofana: 'When the jersey of an Argentinian midfielder, playing in the British Premier League, in a club sponsored by a United Arab Emirates airline, designed by an American kit supplier and produced in China, is worn by an 11-year-old boy in Mali, it becomes a matter of geopolitics. Football mirrors the world's patterns.'[1]

Football shirts may have started out as a piece of equipment to distinguish one team from another, but they have evolved into pieces of currency that immediately communicate to other fans the type of fan or player you might be, or the knowledge you have of the game. An orange 1988 Netherlands shirt worn for a kick-about with friends will reveal your adoration for Rinus Michels' Euros-winning side featuring Ruud Gullit and Ronald Koeman, and Marco van Basten's audacious volley from the silliest of angles to win the final. A 2002 Cameroon vest that was banned by FIFA because of its lack of sleeve, and then worn again with a shirt underneath in an act of protest, might show your general love of a rebel, or simply the striker Samuel Eto'o. A 1978 Coventry shirt, often referred to as the worst-designed kit of all time, is likely to be both laughed at and respected – the shirt would only ever be worn

Football

if the wearer knew the rich story behind it. A football shirt carries cultural legacy, knowledge and optimism in its very fibres.

This evolution of the shirt from equipment to elevated fashion item is physically manifested in the explosion of the 'retro shirt' market. Big brands reference old shirts in their newest releases, talking lovingly about times gone by in their marketing communications. Broadcasting companies such as BT Sport commission shows such as *What I Wore* – a programme that sees an ex-professional working their way through the Classic Football Shirts warehouse to talk about their favourite kits from their career. Football platforms such as MUNDIAL or Panenka tell stories rooted in vintage shirts through editorial in their magazines, social media and on film. YouTube channels are dedicated to 'unboxing' gems from the past, and Instagram and Twitter accounts posting golden nuggets from years gone by amass followers rapidly. A love for a specific shirt is an acknowledgement of what has gone before – a crucial element in a culture where 'knowing your onions' places you in high regard. Most regular customers of companies such as Classic Football Shirts, which sold over 300,000 kits in 2019, will be buying shirts made and played in before they were born.

The continued popularity of the football shirt is not just for professional teams, either. Grassroots clubs and institutions such as Hackney Laces and Romance FC have built on their work in providing safe spaces in the community for all people to play the game through the medium of football shirts. By collaborating with established brands to produce kits for their players, and both physical and online audiences, their shirts represent something more than support for a team – they represent an idea. These teams are crucial to the football pyramid and for the voices of potentially under-represented communities within the game, and the designs of their shirts provide a visible call-out to say that they are here to stay, play and continue to evolve. With the teams' strong online presences, these shirts are quickly snapped up by like-minded football fans from around the world, who challenge the homogeneity and outright commercialism of mainstream competitive football.

The irony of many of these hyper-visible objects is that their designers are largely anonymous. Until a recent spate of high-profile collaborations with designers such as Neville Brody and Wim Crouwel, kit design – specifically football typefaces – was the remit of a small pool of unacknowledged specialists. Key among them is Anthony Barnett, a British designer who worked for ten years at the specialist graphics production company Sporting iD. Producing hundreds of designs for clubs such as AC Milan, Liverpool FC, Galatasaray SK and the Italian national team, Barnett is virtually unknown outside his own small circle. The parameters within which he worked are also obscure to the average football fan, with each letter adhering to strict rules governing sizing, colour contrast and placement while respecting the practical limitations around the printing methods suitable for performance fabrics. Typefaces can't include overhangs, for example, as each letter needs to be individually ironed on to the fabric and the surface can only be melted once. Kits also incorporate a number of anti-counterfeiting devices, such as ultraviolet markings and watermarks. These are hidden within logos and created with highly specialised printing equipment – the invisible foundations of a sprawling and lucrative industry.

Liverpool typeface designed by Anthony Barnett

Football has always been a popular spectator sport. Since the late 1800s, large crowds have gathered to watch matches across the men's and women's game. While the latter is less well known, it was not uncommon for crowds of up to 50,000 to attend women's matches until the FA ban in 1921. This appetite for spectacle led to the development of a very particular piece of public architecture – the

Introduction

Ciao, the mascot for the 1990 FIFA World Cup™

Football

football stadium. The primary purpose of the stadium is to manage crowds, and these highly engineered spaces are best understood as an exercise in choreography. They need to allow huge numbers of people to flow in and out of a space efficiently, safely and in a minimum amount of time. They anticipate, manage and accommodate crowd behaviour, and failure to do so has had tragic consequences in the past. The demands on a stadium are not only practical, however. Many fans compare attending a football match to a religious experience, with stadiums routinely likened to cathedrals or temples. These experiences rely heavily on a sense of procession, ritual and communion, all of which are created by the fans themselves.

The ancient Greeks invented the stadium, and most of what we know about sight lines, flow and acoustics is owed to them. But the specifics of football stadiums stemmed from something far more banal – the invention of a reliable turnstile. In the early days of football spectatorship, crowds would gather on temporary structures, haphazardly erected around the pitch. Few provisions were made, and it was virtually impossible to control or monitor the crowd. All of this changed with the introduction of turnstiles, as clubs were able to count – and charge – their fans, instantly changing their status from supporter to customer. The Salford engineering firm WT Ellison & Co. invented the Rush Preventive Turnstile around 1895, and by the 1930s the majority of large clubs across the UK used this design. The device could process 4,000 entrants per hour, or 3,000 if change had to be sorted, and the distinctive 'clunk' of the machine's turning became a standard part of the matchday ritual. It is no surprise to find that turnstiles featured among the many failures leading to the Hillsborough disaster in 1989, where in certain sections of the stadium 24,256 spectators were expected to pass through just twenty-three turnstiles. Today these devices are largely residual – a small component in the careful monitoring of spectators through the digital technologies that map their journey to and through the stadium. The idea endures, however, and serves as a marker of the fundamental difference between the amateur and professional game.

It cannot be denied that the atmosphere some fans in stadiums have created can be ostracising, intimidating and at times xenophobic. Reflections of the society they are part of, stadiums haven't always been a safe space for huge parts of the population, and because of that, football fans have regularly been tarred with a dark brush. But that characterisation, while sadly true in some instances, misses the brilliant community-led, politically aware and socially conscious work of so many others. Peter Carney's first banner was on the day of Liverpool's FA Cup semi-final replay against Leicester City in 1974, and it was created in a similar vein to most: a yellowing bedsheet with the letters LFC painted on it in massive brushstrokes. Since then, Peter's banners have become synonymous with the Kop End at Liverpool's Anfield stadium, and wherever else they play. Utilising mixed techniques such as silk screen printing, embroidery, painting and appliqué, his displays create a waving sea of red and white, with words that ruminate on politics, ownership, life, death, goals and, of course, Liverpool. Peter, a survivor of the Hillsborough tragedy, was a key campaigner in the subsequent fight for justice, and his original banner was a symbol of unity at a time when the city needed it.

It is impossible to separate the fun, exhilaration and virtuosity of football from its role as a spectacle. Vastly more people watch football than play it, and the basis of this phenomenon is competition. An expansive and intricate cycle of matches has been built up over time, evolving from small local games to major national events and international cup tournaments. These fixtures form the backbone of the football industry, and are the source of its wealth, impact and reach. Without these tournaments, football as we know it would not exist. Football viewership generates enormous amounts of money: European football alone was estimated to hold a value of twenty-two billion pounds in 2016 – a figure that is set to rise.

The planet's biggest football spectacle is of course the FIFA World Cup. World Cups are four-week festivals of football that punctuate the lives of fans through heartbreak, ecstasy and a genuine opportunity to travel to new places. When Italy was awarded the rights to host the 1990 FIFA World Cup, the organisers saw it as an opportunity to provide a modern

Introduction

Subbuteo players, 1975

features a felt pitch and small footballer figurines mounted on semicircular bases, and was long the gaming choice for football fans who wanted to simulate their heroes. The beauty of the game here is not so much in the gameplay – flicking the figurines towards a plastic ball that is around the same height as the players – but rather in the ephemera, and the way a player can create their own dream football situations. With real-life pitches too far away to touch, the players too protected and your own ability never quite enough, watching professional footballers play can seem like looking at another world. Subbuteo allows you to bring that world into your own home with you as the orchestrator, and a mix of official Subbuteo producers and bespoke makers allow you to design this to a baffling level of detail. There are different pitches to choose from, electric floodlights, cameramen, ballboys, a whole spectrum of different plastic stands, individual fans to glue on to terraces, a figure of the Queen for home-made FA Cups, corner flags, balls, commentators, coloured nets, scoreboards, teams. Subbuteo has lived on in different forms over the past eighty years, and since 2020 an official licensed version of the game – now including video assistant referees and television sets – has been available once again. The joy of Subbuteo is in the detailed ways it allows you to live out your own football dreams, whether based in the Africa Cup of Nations, the Scottish Premier League, or a team of your own friends playing against Brazil's 1958 FIFA World Cup winners – the world of football is on your tabletop and at your fingertips.

view of Italy, away from its provincial and archaic stereotype. After the difficulties of the 1980s – with hooliganism rife and a number of horrific stadium disasters – this was an opportunity to show fans in a better light, too. Enter 'Ciao', the futuristic, genderless, cuboid mascot that captured the hearts and imaginations of football fans across the world. The organising committee had run a competition to design the mascot, and after poring over 50,000 entries, it announced a self-taught graphic designer called Lucio Boscardin as the winner. 'I came up with the idea in front of a traffic light,' Boscardin later explained. 'It made me understand that the Italian flag was an element to be valued. I made some simple sketches in my car right there and, in my study, I broke the word "ITALIA" into ten tricolour sticks so that they would become an athlete. Only the head was missing and, inevitably, I put a ball.'[2] Ciao was adored by fans, and lives on through T-shirts, pub discussions, love for the limited-edition 'Ciao' Fiat Panda design, and the iconic photograph of then England manager Sir Bobby Robson leaning on the mascot with a beaming smile. Italian writer Michele Galluzzo later wrote that its popularity stemmed from it being 'detached from historical references',[3] providing a neutral image for fans to project their FIFA World Cup hopes on to.

To contemplate football as a game that only exists on the pitch is not to understand the game at all. It's a game that lives in people's minds, a game that lives on screens through incredibly detailed video games, and a game that even today exists on people's tables. Subbuteo, a tabletop game invented in the 1940s by ex-RAF pilot Peter Adolph,

All of this goes to show that football is the world's most popular sport, and as long as there is the material on the planet to fashion a ball from, it always will be.

1   James Bird, 'Émile-Samory Fofana: Champions League Koulikoro', MUNDIAL, April 2020, www.instagram.com/p/B-fALbzJuxs [accessed 7 December 2021].

2   Sarah Winterburn, 'World Cup Design Classics: Mascot Ciao from 1990', Football365, 19 April 2018, www.football365.com/news/world-cup-design-classics-mascot-ciao-from-1990 [accessed 7 December 2021].

3   Michele Galluzzo, 'The Coordinated Effort to Develop a Coherent Visual Identity for the Italian World Cup', Copa90, 2016, www.copa90.com/en/creators/creator-collective-archive/collective/rivista-undici/2016/1/ciao-italia-90 [accessed 7 December 2021].

1

Performance

Football Boots: A Look at History
Thomas Turner

Specialist sports footwear was a rarity when young British men formalised football in the mid-nineteenth century. But what players wore on their feet was important, and the game placed an unusual combination of demands on players' boots and shoes. Players had to be able to move quickly on a grass pitch, and control, dribble and kick a ball effectively. Their feet also needed protection from the tackles of other players and from the impact of the ball itself. A player's boots or shoes were a crucial interface between them and the playing surface, them and the ball, and, on occasion, them and other players. These basic requirements have endured into the contemporary era, but as the ball, pitch, styles of play and players themselves have changed, so too has players' footwear.

Appropriate footwear is necessary to play football successfully, yet footballers' boots and shoes have a significance that goes beyond the physical. Over time, they have functioned as symbols of wealth and success, and have communicated ideas about gender and class. For the companies that have produced and sold them, football boots have been important consumer goods, with the boots worn by professional players acting as advertisements for wider product ranges.

As mass-produced products, they have been shaped by commercial pressures, by the skills and ingenuity of designers and makers, and by the availability of materials and methods of production. These have always been multipurpose goods, designed to achieve a variety of goals on and off the pitch.

●

The earliest footballers adapted and modified existing footwear styles to suit the needs of the game. During the nineteenth century high-cut boots were worn outdoors by men and women of all social classes, and so boots were commonly pressed into use for playing football. Players at the various public schools that developed the game may also have had special footwear made or adapted by cobblers. For extra traction on muddy surfaces, metal spikes and plates could be fixed to the bottom of leather soled boots, a common practice on walking or work boots. In 1863, the newly formed Football Association felt the need to regulate what players wore on the pitch. Its original rules state that 'No player shall be allowed to wear projecting nails, iron plates, or gutta-percha [a hard natural resin] on the soles or heels of his boots.'[1]

Hand-coloured engraving depicting the Scotland v. England
match of 1872

The Blackburn Olympic team that won the 1883 FA Cup.
Some players are wearing boots with studs, probably made
of leather

That they felt the need to outlaw such practices suggests that the prohibited items – and, one suspects, the violent play that could be associated with them – had been embraced by at least some players seeking to gain an advantage on the pitch.

Early Association Rules players wore a variety of common boot and shoe styles. Photographs and drawings of public school, regimental and local teams in the 1860s and 70s show them in boots with raised heels that are cut just above the ankle bone. They were probably made of leather, and were similar to Victorian formal, work and military boots. William Ralston's illustrations of the first international match, between Scotland and England in Glasgow in 1872, similarly show players in boots, but also several others in what appear to be contemporary lawn tennis shoes. These were made of lightweight leather and had low-cut uppers and flat vulcanised rubber soles that allowed tennis players to move around grass courts quickly without slipping. The massive popularity of lawn tennis in the 1870s and 80s meant these shoes were readily available in shops and department stores, and it was not unusual for them to be used for other games that called for flexible, grippy footwear.[2]

Flat rubber soles may have been satisfactory for dry or hard pitches, but the softer, muddier conditions that were more frequently encountered called for something else. A photograph of the Blackburn Rovers team that won the 1883 FA Cup shows some players wearing boots with studs – probably made of leather – nailed into the soles. These provided a more secure footing on soft ground and soon became the norm. In 1891 the Football Association regulated their use, ruling that studs or bars could be fixed to the bottom of players' footwear, so long as they did not project more than half an inch. Bars had to be at least half an inch wide and extend across the width of the shoe. Studs were required to be round, no less than half an inch in diameter, and not conical or pointed.[3] With this rule change, the football boot as we know it today began to take shape.

Innovation in football boot design was encouraged by the changing nature of footwear production and, from the 1880s onwards, the rise of the professional game. The birth of the Football Association – and the version of the game it established – coincided with a period of industrialisation in the footwear industry. By the 1890s mechanised mass production was the norm among British boot and shoe makers. Newly popular sports like football and lawn tennis provided them with opportunities to adapt existing designs and experiment with new materials and methods of fabrication to create sport-specific styles. Working in relatively new product categories and addressing sporting needs, manufacturers could innovate without the constraints imposed by tradition or previously established products or designs. Moreover, by promoting the use of special shoes for different sporting occasions, manufacturers could encourage the consumption that was necessary to sustain mass production. For many British firms, football boots and other sports footwear became an important source of income. Professional teams had an incentive to provide their players with the best equipment, so manufacturers keen to secure a place in a lucrative market competed with one another to develop boots that gave players a competitive advantage.

The football boots of the 1890s and 1900s conformed to a rough template. The low-cut, flat-soled shoes that had been worn in the 1870s were seemingly forgotten; football was played in boots that were cut above the ankle bone and which were made of cow or calf leather. Leather studs or bars on the sole provided grip, while a tough leather toe cap protected the toes. The similarity to military styles and boots made for manual labour, and the fact that these were boots and not shoes, highlighted the game's significance as an expression of masculinity and reflected the working-class origins of many of the top professional players and teams. For some players, these were indeed work boots. Yet within these broad parameters there existed great variation. Manufacturers patented scores of small technical innovations and gimmicks that were supposed to improve players' abilities, and pseudo-scientific language was frequently deployed in marketing materials. In 1896, the Belgrave Rubber Co. advertised boots that had ankle protectors.[4] In 1906, James Percival and Company offered a boot it called 'The Controller', with a ridged toe cap that supposedly increased a player's ability

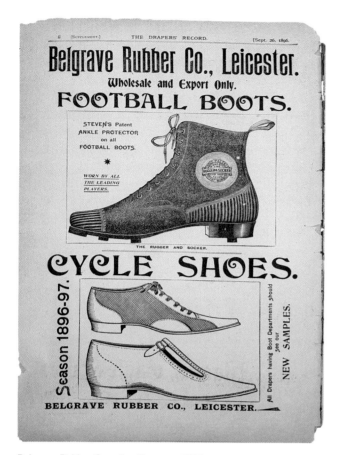

Belgrave Rubber Co. advertisement, 1896

to control the ball.[5] Three years later, Walter, Kempson & Stevens produced boots with rubber ridges on the instep that performed the same function.[6] The leading firms introduced countless variations each season to ensure their boots performed well on the pitch and in the sales rooms of British and overseas retailers. Walter, Kempson & Stevens alone offered sixty different styles in 1909.

Football's popularity as a spectator sport allowed manufacturers to use their links to the professional game to stimulate mass sales. Walter, Kempson & Stevens advertised that its boots were worn by several top players.[7] In the early 1900s M. J. Rice & Son patented a combination stud and bar sole and secured the endorsement of Steve Bloomer, the country's most celebrated striker. 'Steve Bloomer's Lucky Goal Scorers' were sold with the tagline 'When a Past-Master at the Game like STEVE BLOOMER puts the Hall-Mark of his approval on a Football Boot, the Trade and the Public may be sure THAT BOOT IS A GOOD ONE.'[8] The association between Bloomer and the firm continued into the 1940s. Endorsements like these helped sell the boots to a growing

market of schoolboy and amateur players further down the game's hierarchy. Models endorsed by top players were status symbols, of the financial capital needed to buy them but also of commitment, dedication and knowledge about the game.

In Britain, the design orthodoxy established in the late Victorian era lasted well into the twentieth century. Until the 1950s, boots remained high cut, with leather studs and toe caps. Many had a leather strap running across the forefoot, presumably intended to give a clean area to strike the ball, and some included steel stiffeners in the sole. That they provided protection from heavy balls and rough tackles seemed to be their most important characteristic, with grip a close second. The majority of boots in the early 1950s looked very similar to those of three decades or more before. Looking back in 1955, the Football Association wrote that 'boots were something we took very much for granted', and that 'for many years few changes occurred in their design; it was accepted by everyone that they should be heavily built, have re- inforced toes and ankles, and be fitted with the customary type of straps and studs'.[9] To the uninitiated, models like Read, Myall & Read's Hotspur and Walker, Kempson & Stevens' Cert looked almost identical, at least in advertisements.[10]

Beyond Britain, football boots continued to evolve, just as the game itself changed as it spread around the world. Manufacturers began to create footwear suited to their local markets. In South America a more agile,

Advertisement for the Non-Stretch Cert football boot by Walker, Kempson & Stevens, 1909

Football

skilful style of play emerged, and the game began to be played at a faster pace. Players took to wearing low-cut, lightweight boots that hugged the foot and did not have a bulbous toe cap. They looked more like running shoes than traditional workwear and were far lighter than boots made in Britain. At the 1950 FIFA World Cup in Brazil, Stanley Matthews, a key member of England's World Cup squad, was so impressed that he bought himself a pair in a Rio sports shop and later asked the Co-operative Wholesale Society (CWS), one of Britain's largest boot manufacturers, to copy them. Shortly after, a Stanley Matthews range that incorporated many of their features was introduced to Britain. The new models were advertised with a promise to 'streamline a player's speed, put an edge to his skill, and cut out foot fatigue'. Over half a million pairs were sold in the early 1950s at Co-op stores around Britain.[11]

The game developed in a similar direction in continental Europe. During the 1930s in Germany, the sports shoe company owned by Adolf and Rudolf Dassler, the brothers who in the late 1940s founded adidas and Puma, similarly created lightweight boots to enable faster play. Adolf Dassler was an amateur player and knew that most of a match was spent running, not kicking the ball, and that heavy footwear increased fatigue. In the early 1950s his new company, adidas, started working closely with the West German football federation and produced a range of technically innovative boots that were far lighter and more flexible than those made in Britain. The firm also introduced boots with screw-in synthetic studs. This meant a pair of boots could be made to last longer, as worn studs could be replaced more easily, but also that the studs could be changed to suit different ground conditions: shorter studs for hard ground, longer for soft ground. The 1954 FIFA World Cup provided a chance to showcase these developments on a world stage. It was the first post-war tournament to admit a German team and the first to be broadcast extensively. Dassler accompanied the West German squad through the competition to their surprise win over the favourites, Hungary, in a rain-soaked final. The victory was popularly ascribed to Dassler's late decision to change the team's studs to suit the wet pitch, and more generally to the superiority of their footwear. Dassler was dubbed 'der Schuh-Marschall' by the West German press, his products symbolic of German post-war revival and technical ingenuity. The company exploited the publicity, which generated global interest in its products. Business roughly doubled in the following year, and by 1961 adidas was the largest producer of football boots in the world.[12]

During the 1950s, boots like those developed in South America and Germany gradually became the norm. Seeing the popularity and success of adidas – and encouraged by a chastened English Football Association, reeling from defeats against Hungary – British manufacturers launched low-cut 'Continental' styles of their own. At the same time, football boots were transformed by the introduction and use of new oil-based plastics. adidas was a pioneer in this respect and worked closely with West German chemical and machine companies to produce football boots with rubber and nylon soles. These offered a weight

Adolf (Adi) Dassler (1900–78), photographed in the late 1950s with a boot featuring screw-in studs

advantage over leather and had the benefit of not becoming soaked with moisture in wet conditions, and so not becoming heavier as the game progressed. Moulded rubber and plastic soles also allowed the stud pattern to be changed, and adidas offered multi-studded models suited to drier conditions. Some firms, notably Stylo Matchmakers in Britain, experimented with plastic uppers, but in general leather, sometimes padded with synthetic foam, remained the most popular upper material.[13] For the most expensive boots, adidas and some other manufacturers used kangaroo skin, a leather known for its lightness and flexibility. These developments in footwear were accompanied by gradual changes to the ball, which over time became lighter, meaning the need for foot protection was reduced.

The 1950s also saw the aesthetic transformation of football boots. Until this point, most football boots tended to be uniform black or brown, and from afar most looked the same. This was all changed by the arrival and success of adidas, which branded its black boots with three distinctive white stripes. Rudolf Dassler's Puma added a curved white stripe to its boots. Although adidas said publicly that the stripes provided support, in effect they were a clever marketing device that made adidas products instantly recognisable. With the advent of television and increased media coverage of elite football and other sports, the stripes meant the boots worn by professional players became advertisements for the wider range of adidas products. adidas and Puma gave away vast quantities of boots to professional players and in the 1960s began to pay them to wear their products. Newspaper, magazine and television pictures cemented their connection to the elite and brought their products to a global audience. Seeing the success of the German firms, other companies were quick to launch branding devices of their own, and from the mid-1950s football boots were increasingly decorated with a range of distinctive flashes and stripes.

Football boots also gradually became more colourful. In the 1960s adidas introduced black boots with a distinctive blue rubber sole and others with blue linings. It also produced a range of flat-soled training shoes

in brightly coloured soft leathers. The Danish company Hummel brought out a range of coloured boots and paid top professionals to wear them. During the 1970s there was a fashion for increasingly elaborate brand marks in fluorescent colours on the sides of boots.[14] Nevertheless, the main body of most boots remained black. Although the main body of most boots remained black, the gradual creep of colour into football boot design represented a qualified engagement with the peacock fashions that in the 1960s and 70s were transforming male dress – and ideas of masculinity – away from sport.

●

By the 1960s it was established that football boots should have lightweight black leather uppers, visible branding and synthetic studded soles. Although manufacturers introduced countless improvements and changes in the years that followed, this basic model stayed in place until the end of the 1990s. The contemporary era began with the launch by Nike of the Mercurial R9, a silver and blue, fully synthetic, extremely lightweight boot worn by the Brazilian star Ronaldo at the 1998 FIFA World Cup. During the 2000s, leather finally gave way to synthetic materials, with the development of new knitting technologies

Nike Mercurial, Nike, 1998–

Football

transforming boots into something similar to slippers or socks. Lighter balls and more stringent refereeing of violent challenges meant boots needed to provide less protection. More uniform pitches, especially at the highest level, and greater research into movement and ergonomics meant studs evolved into a pattern of blades that facilitated quick changes of direction. The introduction of materials like carbon fibre provided rigidity while reducing weight. The sober black of the previous era gave way to an eye-catching riot of colours, as new synthetic materials allowed manufacturers to draw on a far wider palette to make their boots instantly recognisable. The rise, too, of the women's game meant boot manufacturers finally took their needs into consideration, and ranges of boots designed for women began to emerge.

●

If we look to the future, it seems more changes will be needed. The earliest boots were made of natural materials – leather, cotton and steel – by small firms or individual craftspeople. Today's boots are hybrids of oil-based plastics, almost entirely synthetic constructions, made and sold in vast numbers by global sporting goods companies. As the world becomes aware of the growing problem of plastic waste and the environmental impact of the clothing industry, the unsustainability of the current model of production and consumption becomes increasingly apparent. Once again, designers and makers may need to look to new materials and production processes that can transform the material reality of the football boot. Innovation and ingenuity should be focused on the ways in which football boots can be made, repaired and replaced without negatively impacting the natural world that is so necessary for the game itself.

1 Ebenezer Cobb Morley, *Laws of the Game: On Behalf of the Football Association*. Quoted in Jean Williams, 'Given the Boot: Reading the Ambiguities of British and Continental Football Boot Design', in Jean Williams (ed.), *Kit: Fashioning the Sporting Body* (London: Routledge, 2015), p. 83.

2 Thomas Turner, *The Sports Shoe: A History from Field to Fashion* (London: Bloomsbury, 2019), pp. 14–41.

3 John Simkin, 'Football Boots', Spartacus Educational, spartacus-educational.com/Fboots.htm [accessed 7 January 2022].

4 Belgrave Rubber Co. advertisement, *The Drapers' Record*, 26 September 1896, supplement, p. ii.

5 James Percival and Company advertisement, *The Shoe and Leather Record*, 23 March 1906, supplement, pp. lxxviii–lxxix.

6 'For Footballers', *The Shoe and Leather Record*, 26 March 1909, p. 629.

7 Walker, Kempson & Stevens Ltd advertisement, *The Shoe and Leather Record*, 26 March 1909, supplement, pp. lxx–lxxi.

8 M. J. Rice & Son advertisement, *The Shoe and Leather Record*, 5 February 1909, pp. 260–261.

9 'Boots in the Backroom', in *The Football Association Year Book 1955–1956* (London: William Heinemann, 1955), pp. 77–78.

10 Read, Myall & Read advertisement in Williams, 'Given the Boot', p. 90; Walker, Kempson & Stevens advertisement in *The Shoe*

and Leather News, 1 June 1934, p. 53.

11 Stanley Matthews, *The Way It Was: My Autobiography* (London: Headline, 2000), pp. 236–238; Co-operative Wholesale Society advertisement, *Charles Buchan's Football Monthly*, September 1951, back cover; Co-operative Wholesale Society advertisement, *The Shoe and Leather Record*, 5 August 1954, p. 41; 'Letter to the Editor: Lightweight Football Boots', *The Shoe and Leather Record*, 29 September 1955, p. 226.

12 Christian Kleinschmidt, 'The Other "Miracle of Bern". The Rise of adidas and Brand-oriented Management After the Second World War', in Rainer Karlsch, Christian Kleinschmidt, Jörg Lesczenski and Anne Sudrow, *Playing the Game: The History of adidas* (Munich: Prestel, 2018),

pp. 86–95; Keith Cooper, *adidas: The Story As Told By Those Who Have Lived It and Are Living It* (Herzogenaurach: adidas, 2011), pp. 28–72; Barbara Smit, *Pitch Invasion: Three Stripes, Two Brothers, One Feud: adidas and the Making of Modern Sport* (London: Allen Lane, 2006), pp. 45–58.

13 'George Best insisted on working on every facet of design of Stylo boots which bear his name', *The Shoe and Leather News*, 1 January 1970, p. 33.

14 'Fluorescent flashes brighten soccer shoe "fashion scene"', *The Shoe and Leather News*, 14 December 1972, pp. 18–19.

The Revolution Will Be Rubberised
Sam Handy

When adidas launched the first Predator boot in 1994, the world of football had seen nothing like it. By adding shallow rubber shelves to the upper and outsole, adidas promised a boot that would provide footballers with more control when they struck a football: a boot that, according to their marketing, was '100% legal, 0% fair'. This was an earthquake in a market that had stuck to what it knew for so long, and the brand knows that it must build on this with each new iteration of the boot. Sam Handy, VP Design/Running at adidas, tells us what it's like to work on a bona fide design revolution …

●

The first boot really to change what people thought a football boot could do, from both a playing and a manufacturing perspective, was the adidas Copa Mundial. The screw-in studs that Adi Dassler created to use in different weather conditions were revolutionary, and the 'Miracle of Bern', when the West German national side wore them in muddy conditions and utilised the different studs, is a very physical example of that. The next big innovation was Predator. Prior to this, everything was still a classically stitched leather football boot, and the idea of adding rubber grips to give more ball control, more swerve and better ball manipulation was a huge change. Lots of things came off the back of that change, like bladed studs and carbon plates, but the big innovation was this movement from quilted leather to a hybrid leather with a grip on top of it.

I work with a lot of professional footballers, and it's very difficult to get them to change their boot. They're essentially never looking for the next big thing in boots because they're so superstitious, and if they've got something they feel comfortable in and it's working for them, they're very hesitant to change it. You've seen that with so many elite players who barely change their boots during their career. So, it's the role of a performance innovation brand like adidas to investigate and find a way that their game can be improved. They'll only ever change if we make something that genuinely improves their game, and that difference is made in the sports science research and the materials research.

David Beckham once told a story about the first time he saw someone playing in a Predator, and how he remembered thinking 'I've got to get myself a pair of those. Let me try them on.' Once you see a pro or peer playing in something that's clearly giving them an edge, a stone drops and you see a ripple effect. The design innovation was something that was easy to understand: this product lets me grip the ball better in the place where I kick the ball. It's a really simple, linear, easy-to-comprehend design. From a player perspective, if you've ever kicked a football, you know that getting more grip at contact will help you control it better.

When adidas took the Predator off the market in 2015, it was because the boot had become too similar to its competitors. And so, when I started working in football, it was a football with no Predator. I missed it as soon as I started.

We were kicking off things for the FIFA World Cup in 2018, and I remember saying, 'Surely we need to use the platform of the next World Cup to bring back the best franchise in football.' As much as there were people who loved the idea, there were lots of others who said, 'No, we need to move on, you can't go backwards.' My argument was that when you have an iconic product like a Predator, it's timeless, and if you build the best-performance Predator you've ever done, then the name Predator doesn't make it old.

So we created the new boot, the Predator 18, with things like a brand-new knit forefront and a ribbed control zone at the front that was part of the boot and not made of rubber.

adidas Predator, 1994

The Revolution Will Be Rubberised

The first thing everyone does with a new boot is the 'thumb test', and I think that boot with the ribs had a really special material on top of the prime.

These boots are a very ageless concept. There are as many people in their forties and fifties who are in love with the Predator as there are people in their twenties and younger. I'll use Paul Pogba as an example. In 2016, we did a Juergen Teller photoshoot with Paul ahead of the Euros, and I was in his house. For Juergen, Paul pulled out his boot collection and in it were all of these iconic, mid–1990s Predator colourways. It was very powerful, and made me think 'OK, you're a young, elite professional footballer at the very top of the game, and you've just pulled out your own Predator collection.' I knew at that point that the relaunch would be a slam dunk. And it turned out to be the case that whenever we showed that new Predator to professional players, you'd just see their eyes change. And now that we're working on the new iterations, it's a similar thing. It's a shoe that gives people sparkly eyes, somehow.

We're now at the stage where the relaunches are being revolutionised, and if you hold the evolution of the new shoes in your hand, Predator 18 through to 20, you see a linear change where they are becoming better performance products. We brought in the Primeknit and the rubber back, something people felt was missing from the first relaunch, with the 406 individual rubber Demonskin spikes for that grip. It's difficult to work on an icon, where people are saying the original is the best, don't touch it, don't relocate, but it's more 'I don't want to break it, I just want to evolve it.'

That happened recently, in late 2021, with the vegan Predator that Paul Pogba made in collaboration with Stella McCartney. Never would I have expected, all those years ago, that adidas would make the first vegan shoe, and that it would be praised. Typically, you'd think it's the brutal, tough, aggressive boot, and lo and behold, it's the world's first vegan football shoe. It's surprising, interesting, perhaps even something that looks counterintuitive, and very cool.

And that, for me, is how it started. A classic football boot with everything better from the future added to it.

Sam Handy was interviewed by James Bird

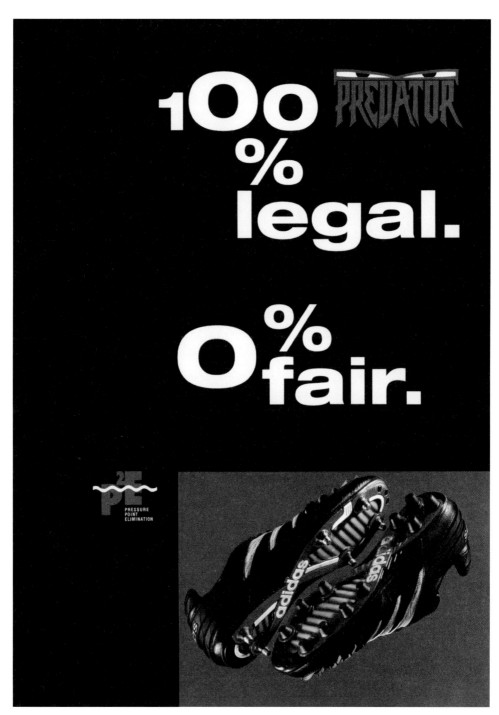

Page from the adidas trade catalogue 1994–5

A View from the Pitch:

A Game-Changer
Iqra Ismail

Iqra Ismail is the Director of Women's Football at grassroots club Hilltop FC in northwest London, and a bona fide football pioneer. Iqra played football on the streets and in the playground from a young age, but didn't join a club until she was fourteen. After playing for the youth teams of various professional sides, and then her university team in Portsmouth, Iqra headed back to London to set up her own club, where she organised, played and coached.

In 2019 Iqra was messaged on Twitter by a woman who worked for the Somali Cultural Society, who asked if she'd be interested in being part of the first ever Somali Women's National Team. And a couple of months later, on a pitch in Cape Town, Iqra led the side out as captain. After years of civil war, national and international turmoil, and a cultural situation that made it difficult for women to play, it was time to let football do the talking. Here, Iqra tells us about her experiences with the Nike Pro hijab.

●

The first time I saw the Nike Pro hijab, I felt like it was something I didn't really need. I'd spent so long playing football with my normal, everyday hijab that I just wasn't sure what impact it would have on my game. Maybe I didn't realise the full functionality of it because it was something I'd never had access to before.

But the first time I tried it on – wow. I remember it vividly. Immediately, I was wondering how I managed before. It was a completely different experience, and it made me feel more like an athlete, rather than feeling like I'm an athlete who wears a hijab. It instantly felt like part of my kit, rather than an addition to it. The hijab was constructed from a material that had a similar feel to all of my other performance clothing, so from the moment I put it on, it just felt right.

The product changed my game straight-away. It meant I could stop thinking about so many things that I shouldn't have to think about to play football. Like the way I would have to style my everyday hijab before the game so that it wouldn't fall off, or thinking about taking valuable minutes out at half-time to fix it rather than concentrate on what I needed to do in the second half, or thinking

about shifting back every time I headed the ball so that I could fix it straight after – all of that kind of stuff was suddenly just out of the window. It removed a lot of worries that weren't directly related to the football, and it gave me an opportunity to focus more on my game rather than having to make sure that my religion wasn't compromised while I was playing.

It felt special, because it made me feel like there are other Muslim athletes. It had always felt like there weren't so many of us and therefore the market wasn't big enough to design such a product. But with this, there was something to improve the game for Muslim footballers, Muslim taekwondo athletes, Muslim MMA fighters, cricketers, whatever. We now have a part of our kit that allows us to participate without having to worry.

It gave a whole different level of inclusivity and a feeling of being part of the game.

Iqra Ismail was interviewed by James Bird, photograph by Hamish Stephenson for Nike Football

A View from the Pitch

A View from the Pitch:

The Man in the Middle
Nathan Buckle

A proper football match simply cannot exist without referee to interpret and enforce the 'Laws of the Game'. The pressure on this person to make what players on both sides deem the correct decision is extraordinarily high, whether they are officiating the Champions League final in front of 90,000 people at Camp Nou or reffing a game on a local park between twenty-two players, a couple of hungover substitutes, and a man walking his dog. There is, without doubt, a blame culture within football – from the elite game to grassroots – that needs to change. Frustrations must move away from being aimed at refereeing decisions.

Referees do the job because they love the game, and Nathan Buckle, a thirty-three-year-old from East London who referees on the iconic Hackney Marshes alongside other grassroots leagues in the area, is no different.

●

I started refereeing when I was twenty-three after injuries cut short my playing days. Being a coach or a manager on the sidelines, you're part of the game, but as a referee, you're on the pitch. Right in the middle of every single action.

You get to feel the vibe and atmosphere from everyone involved: the manager, the players, the fans watching. I've always told people that being a referee you get the best view of the best goals. And that was my main reason for starting out as a referee – you've got the best seat in the house.

Referees do get a lot of stick and abuse, and it's there at every level. It's so easy to criticise the referee and to blame them for your team losing a game, and therefore you don't hear referees speak a lot in the media, because as soon as they say one thing that could be perceived as wrong, there'd be even more reason to scrutinise them.

But I love refereeing. Every single element of every single game is different. You're constantly stimulated, and it keeps you mentally fit because you can't lose focus for a second. In every game you play you meet different characters, and you're in a position where you're constantly having to explain why you have made a certain decision or not taken a certain action, and I like to manage situations like this.

The whistle is part of the essential kit for a referee, but it shouldn't be something that

you rely on; it's something you should use with care. The most valuable piece of kit on the pitch is your mouth and your hand signals. You need to constantly talk to players on the pitch, and then use hand signals to communicate to those who can't hear you. It's your mouth that gives you match control, and the whistle aids that, alongside your cards. I try to use it as little as possible, using my mouth to communicate things that happen regularly such as a goal kick, and if I use the whistle it's because I need everyone to know that something has happened and I need to take control. The whistle is a powerful tool to be used with caution.

For me, presentation is everything and I've got to turn up at the pitch looking correct. Your representation of your county affiliate for refereeing, and for your society of referees, is important. I'd never turn up with badges that are hanging off my shirt or dirty socks. As soon as the players see you in your kit, they know you're the referee, and that first impression is so important for what happens in the rest of the game.

Whether you're doing it for fun or for fitness, you've always got to treat refereeing as a profession, and there always has to be an air of responsibility about everything you do.

Nathan Buckle was interviewed by James Bird, photograph by Alan Bond

A View from the Pitch

Harrow School ball, 1800s

Although the origins of football are disputed, the game as we know it today evolved out of Britain's elite public schools, where different forms of the sport developed with their own rules and styles of equipment. At Harrow School in northwest London, this heavy ball made from an animal bladder enclosed in thick leather, would have been dribbled, kicked and caught in a muddy field. The materials could withstand the conditions, but would increase in weight as they absorbed water and were therefore not suited to heading.

Football

Football made from maize meal sack,
tied with string, Zambia, 2011

Lillywhites Gentlemen's Boots, of the type worn by Corinthians, Lillywhites, 1890s

Girl's boots, worn to play football, 1890

Pair of 'Cup Tie' boots with reinforced strap, c.1910

In the 1800s, men and women played football wearing leather work boots. They were a very high cut, sometimes with reinforced toecap made from steel, which was designed to withstand working conditions. These features made them suitable for kicking the large and heavy balls used at the time. A similar style of boot was worn by members of English amateur football club Corinthian (active from 1882 to 1939), which is believed to have popularised the game around the world and was famed for its high regard for sportsmanship and fair play.

Football

Arsenal boot room at Highbury, 1951

Match ball from the 1930 FIFA World
Cup™ final, supplied by Argentina, 1930

Match ball from the 1930 FIFA World
Cup™ final, supplied by Uruguay, 1930

The FIFA World Cup, international
football's foremost tournament, was first
held in 1930. The final, between Argentina
and Uruguay, took place at the Estadio
Centenario in Montevideo, Uruguay.
Mistrust on both sides meant that a
different ball was used for each half of
the match. Argentina supplied a 12-panel
ball for the first half, and took a 2-1 lead.
Uruguay swapped this for an 11-panel
T-model ball for the second half, beating
Argentina 4-2 and making them the first
ever winners of the World Cup.

Football

Superball advertisement, 1931

Patented in 1931 in Argentina by
Romano Polo, Antonio Tossolini and
Juan Valbonesi, the Superball was the
first football without a large leather
seam, inflated using a small air-valve.
The absence of leather laces improved
the design as it meant that the ball
was less painful to head. This led to
it being universally adopted.

Performance

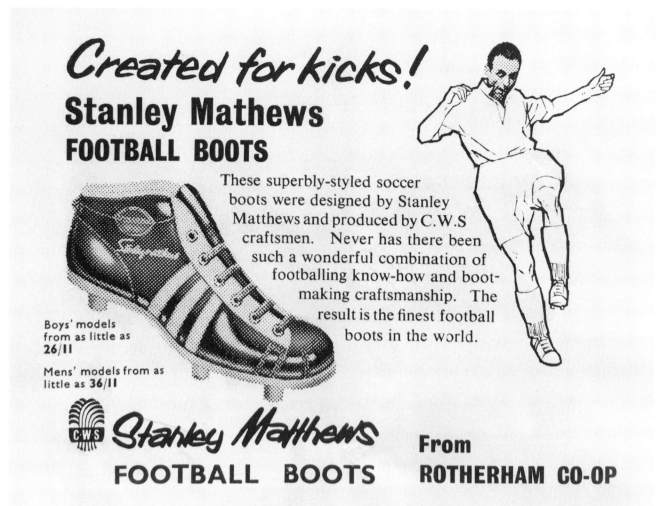
Advertisement for Stanley Matthews football boots, 1950s

In the 1930s, a lower cut boot emerged in southern Europe and South America. It was an important design innovation. Different styles of play, including dribbling and elaborate footwork, had developed in these warmer climates, where football was played on drier, harder pitches with less mud. This so-called 'Continental' style boot was popularised in the UK in the 1950s by celebrated England footballer Stanley Matthews. In collaboration with the Co-operative Wholesale Society, he designed a pair for the mass market that offered flexible, lightweight soles and free ankle movement.

Football

George Best's first pair of football
boots, c.1960

Considered one of the sport's finest
players, Northern Irish footballer
George Best was given these boots when
he joined his first youth team, Cregagh
Boys. On the sides in white paint, he
recorded details of the games in which
he scored goals. Best took the boots
with him when he joined Manchester
United in 1961.

Performance

Puma Super-Atom, Puma, 1952

The late 1940s was a time of unprecedented innovation in football equipment, which was in great part down to German siblings Adolf and Rudolf Dassler. They first manufactured footwear together as Gebrüder Dassler Schuhfabrik, but split in the late 1940s, with Rudolf forming Puma and Adolf forming adidas. Puma released the revolutionary Super-Atom, thought to be the first boot with screw-in studs. Designed in collaboration with West Germany's national coach Josef Herberger, it was initially available only to players in the top division of Germany's national league, the Bundesliga.

Football

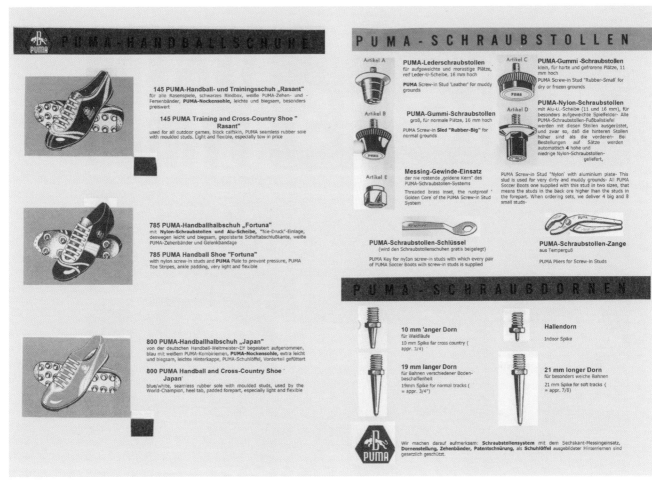

Puma trade catalogue, Puma, 1957

Puma 'formstrip' patent, Puma, 1959

Performance

adidas+WM66

20 Spieler im Finale mit adidas
20 players in the final with adidas

Weltmeister England
World Cup Winner England
Vize-Weltmeister Deutschland
The second: Germany

Players wearing adidas boots at the
1966 FIFA World Cup™ final, 1966

adidas Argentinia, adidas, 1954

Like Puma, adidas was instrumental in setting new standards for elite football equipment. This boot was worn by the West German team at the 1954 FIFA World Cup in Bern, Switzerland. The screw-in studs could be adjusted in length, giving the players the advantage of greater ball control and running speed on a wet pitch. When the underdogs of the tournament, West Germany, beat the favourites, Hungary, in the final, the match became known as the 'Miracle of Bern'.

Performance

Launched in 1968, the Puma King was
designed in honour of Mozambican-
born Portuguese player Eusébio da Silva
Ferreira. A boot featuring a flexible
sole and lightweight nylon screw studs,
the King has been in production for
more than fifty years. It has been worn
by some of history's greatest players,
including Argentina's Diego Maradona
and the Netherlands' Johan Cruyff.
Brazilian legend Edson Arantes do
Nascimento, better known as Pelé,
wore a bespoke version with a yellow
'formstrip' for his fourth FIFA World Cup
in 1970.

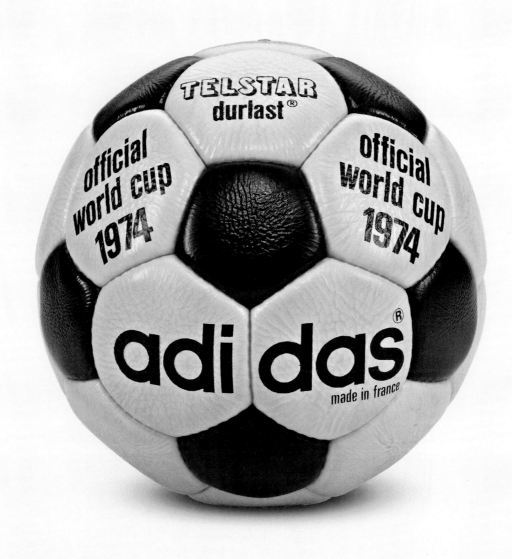

adidas Telstar, adidas, 1974

Comprising thirty-two panels of white hexagons and black pentagons, the Telstar design has become the archetype for modern footballs. The idea of designing a ball in this form came from Danish goalkeeper Eigil Nielsen. The ball was named after a US communications satellite, with the design and colours intended to make the ball easily visible on television. It was used for the first time during the 1970 FIFA World Cup, having been commissioned by FIFA as the official match ball.

Performance

adidas Copa Mundial, designed 1979, produced 1993

An iconic boot of the 1980s, worn by many great players, the Copa Mundial remains in production and largely unchanged today. The boot's name is Spanish for 'World Cup', as it was released for the 1982 tournament in Spain. It features a fold-over tongue, a relatively heavy soleplate with twelve conical studs, and a lightweight kangaroo leather upper.

BOTTOM

Matthias Sammer's customised football boots, 1994

The 1990s saw the start of player endorsement by major sports brands. German footballer Matthias Sammer was under a deal with adidas for the 1994/5 season, but his club, Borussia Dortmund, was sponsored by the competing brand Nike. Sammer insisted on playing in his own shoes and covered the adidas trademark three stripes with a handmade Nike logo. A player's association with certain boot brands and models continues to have the power – as their fame increases – to drive billions of pounds worth of sales.

Football

adidas Jabulani, adidas, 2010

Launched at the 2010 FIFA World Cup
in South Africa, the Jabulani ball
was developed in partnership with
researchers at Loughborough University
to be more aerodynamic. It is made of
just eight thermally bonded 3D synthetic
panels and features a 'grip and groove'
surface for better boot contact.
Players found the ball's movement
unpredictable, however, and its use
in the tournament was considered
controversial by many.

Performance

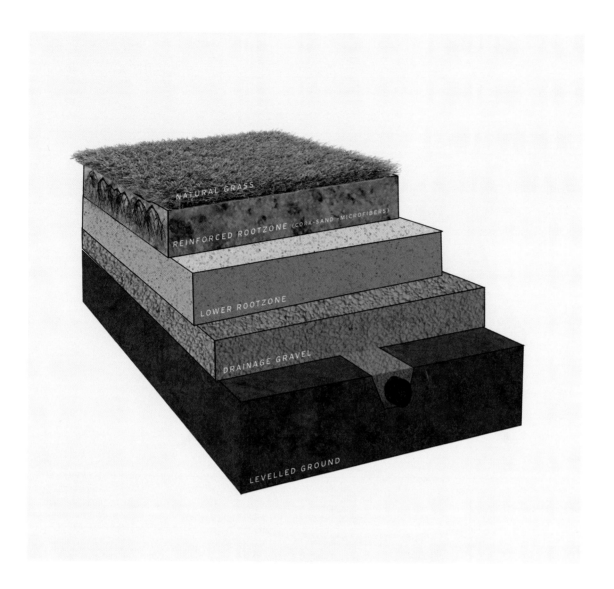

NATURAL GRASS

REINFORCED ROOTZONE (CORK-SAND-MICROFIBERS)

LOWER ROOTZONE

DRAINAGE GRAVEL

LEVELLED GROUND

Cross-section of hybrid turf,
Natural Grass

Football boots are designed in relation
to their playing surface, and as new
technologies and materials have been
developed, the pitch itself has become
a highly technical and engineered piece
of design. The illusion of naturally
occurring, perfectly green turf seen in
stadiums is produced and maintained
by a small army of experts. Today
there are three main styles of turf:
natural, artificial and hybrid. Hybrid
pitches are made from natural grass
combined with synthetic. This turf style
is predominantly used in professional
environments and has had an impact
on the game itself, making it faster while
minimising the risk of injury.

Football

adidas Ace 16+ Purecontrol SG made for
Julian Draxler, Primeknit, adidas, 2016

This boot is completely laceless and
therefore designed with a larger surface
area to create the cleanest possible
strike. The upper is constructed from
a single knitted textile using Primeknit
technology, forming a sock around the
foot. As football is played at a faster
speed than ever before, on near perfect
pitches, there is less demand for boots
to play a protective role.

Performance

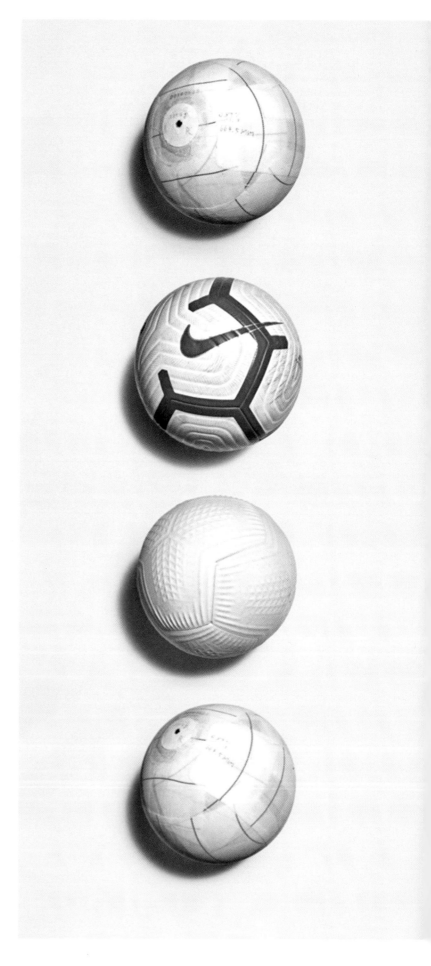

Nike Flight, Nike, 2020

The Flight is the product of eight years of research and testing, with Nike claiming the ball has a thirty per cent 'truer flight'. As a ball moves through space, air grips its surface, slowing it down and causing changes in direction. This football consists of only four panels and is covered in an aerodynamic geometric pattern of grooves, called AerowSculpt.

Football

Performance

'Frankenshoe' prototype, Ida Sports, 2018

The Ida Classica, Ida Sports, 2020

Gender biases in society mean women's football has historically been either neglected or banned completely. Men and women have different physical requirements, and a lack of tailored designs in football equipment has been a factor hindering fair participation in the sport. Dedicated brands are now focusing exclusively on women's football. Australia's Ida Sports has spent several years developing a boot for women, with a narrower heel, wider forefoot and higher arch. This early prototype was tested and refined using feedback from players.

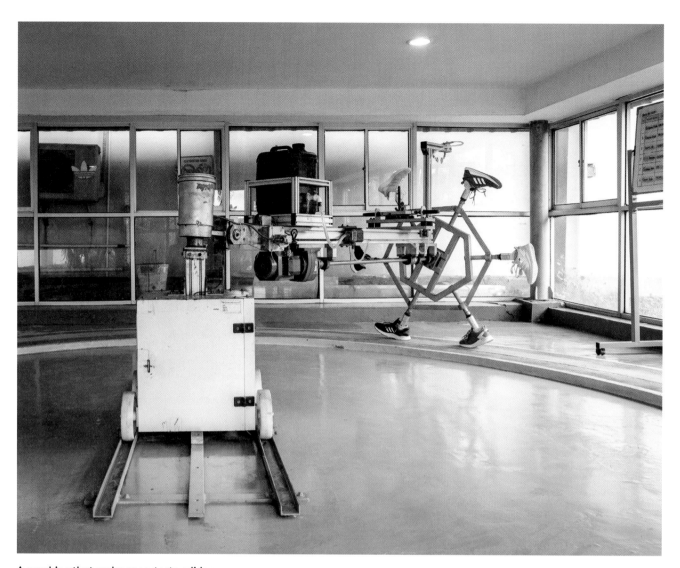

A machine that endurance-tests adidas
shoes at the factory, Indonesia

Inside adidas, Alastair Philip Wiper,
2017

In this series of photographs, British
artist Alastair Philip Wiper documents
how new materials and concepts
are tested by robots in the research
department at the adidas headquarters
in Herzogenaurach, Germany. His
images also provide a portal into the
factories across the world that produce
tens of thousands of products a day.

Football

A machine to test football boots at
adidas' Future Sports Science Lab,
Germany

Performance

Part of a machine that produces adidas
shoes, Germany

Football

adidas shoes in a lasting machine,
Germany

adidas shoe lasts in the prototyping
department, Germany

58

The fabric and cut of football kits is constantly adapted to afford players increased speed and comfort. Advances in material technologies and manufacturing techniques have led to high-performance fabrics that are ever lighter and more breathable. This selection of England shirts demonstrates the progression of design from long-bodied cotton or flannelette to crewneck cotton. More recently, with the rise of synthetic fabrics such as elastane, shirt design has focused on ventilation and sweat-wicking fabrics to regulate body temperature.

OPPOSITE TOP

England 1950 FIFA World Cup™ shirt, worn by Len Shackleton, St Blaize, c.1950

OPPOSITE BOTTOM

England 1966 FIFA World Cup™ shirt, issued to George Eastham, Umbro, 1966

RIGHT TOP

England 1982 FIFA World Cup™ shirt, belonging to Bryan Robson, Admiral, 1980-2

RIGHT BOTTOM

England 2020 national shirt, Nike, 2018

Performance

‘Famous English Football Players’,
print from *The Boy's Own Paper*, 1881

Football can be a dangerous sport and
various pieces of equipment have been
designed to prevent injury. Originating in
cricket, shinpads were first introduced to
football in 1874. Their invention is credited
to the cricketer and footballer Sam Weller
Widdowson, who is shown in this print,
sixth from the left in the back row.

Shinpads, 1890s

Early shinpads were worn outside a
player's socks. They were made from
leather and stuffed with animal hair
for padding. Shinpads started to be
worn under socks in the 1900s and have
become smaller over time as players
prioritised speed and agility over
personal protection.

Performance

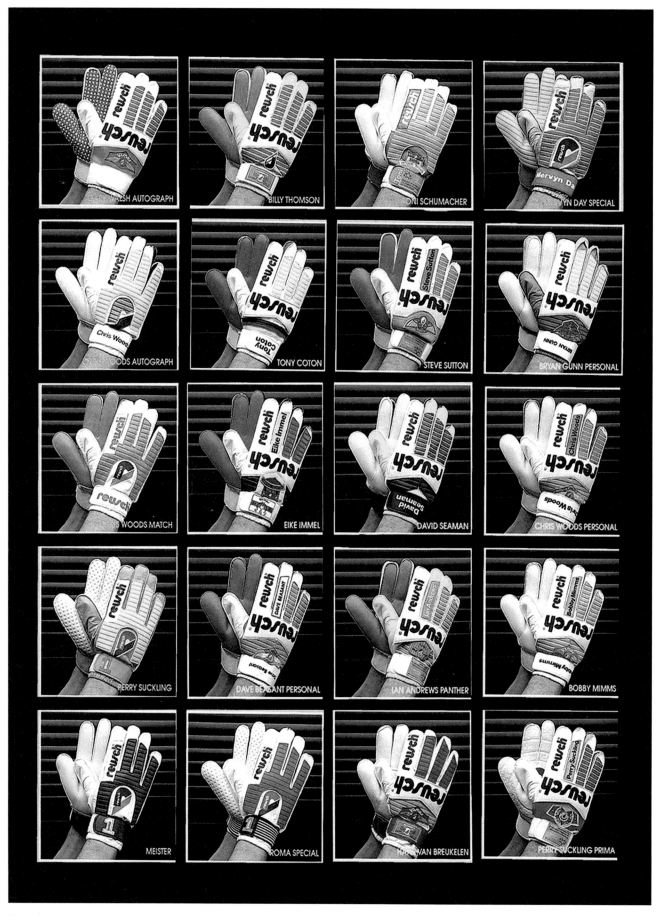

Reusch gloves, Reusch, 1988–9

Football

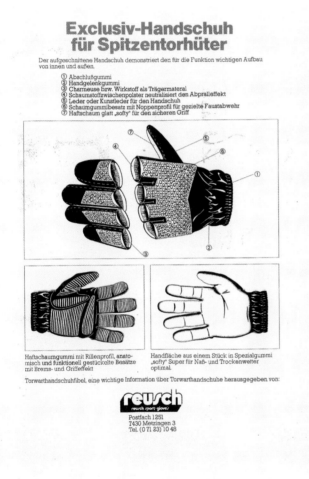

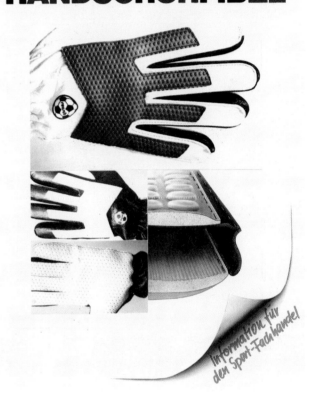

Reusch catalogue, c.1975

German ski-glove manufacturer
Reusch has played an important part
in developing goalkeeping gloves into a
key piece of equipment. Their first pair
was created in collaboration with Sepp
Maier, goalkeeper for West Germany's
national team, and based on a rubber
surgical glove. Over the years, the
brand has experimented and developed
multiple types of palm padding that
increase grip and durability.

Performance

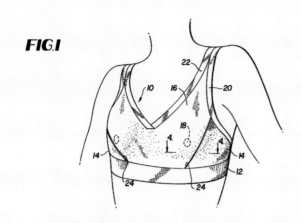

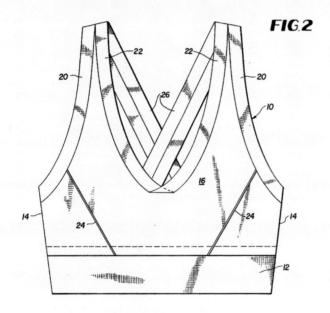

'Jogbra' patent, 1978

Specially designed bras are a necessary protective garment for women to wear during sport. This is especially true for football, where athletes can be subjected to repeated blows to the chest. The first dedicated sports bra was invented for jogging in 1978 by Lisa Lindahl, Polly Smith and Hinda Schreiber. Today, sports bras are still a developing area of study, with leading sportswear brands making efforts to design comfortable yet supportive models.

Nike Pro hijab, Nike, 2017

In 2017, Nike developed a single-layer
stretchy hijab suitable for sports
performance. It was designed to
help make sport more inclusive and
accessible for Muslim women. In cultures
and countries where barriers exist
between exercise and religion, designs
such as this can help to inspire and
empower more women to participate.
In 2007, FIFA enforced a ban on
headwear on the basis that the risk
of injury was too high. After mounting
pressure and campaigning, the ban
was eventually lifted in 2014.

Performance

The humble whistle is one of the
referee's fundamental tools. In 1884,
Birmingham toolmaker Joseph Hudson
invented the first sports whistle,
the Acme Thunderer, which is still in
production today. It was the world's first
'pea' whistle, where a small piece of cork
is inserted inside the whistle to make the
sound more distinguishable, and its snail
shape is ideal for holding in the hand.

Performance

Preston Ladies FC (formerly known
as Dick, Kerr Ladies) captain Lily Parr
explains tactics to her team, 1939

When taking a rising or falling ball, Leon Leuty uses his body to cushion the impact, prevent a heavy rebound and thus bring the ball immediately under control. Notice how the arms are kept away from the ball.

With a bouncing ball he checks his forward run and arches his body, sloping it downwards from the hips. He takes the ball into the lower part of the chest, drawing in slightly at the contact to get a cushioning effect. As the ball falls to the ground he is ready to move away quickly with the ball at his feet.

With a dropping ball Leon holds his head backwards and arches his back slightly, swaying backwards and bending his knees at the moment of impact. He takes the ball on the top of his chest. Again, he is ready to move away with the ball as soon as it falls.

When jumping for the ball, Leon rides backwards as the ball makes contact. This prevents the ball bouncing hard off his chest and brings it down to his feet under control. He can often confuse an opponent by jumping as if to head a ball, and instead take it on his chest

WORLD COPYRIGHT RESERVED

PRODUCED FOR THE FOOTBALL ASSOCIATION BY EDUCATIONAL PRODUCTIONS LTD.

Football Association coaching sheets
Football Association, 1940s

The principles of coaching were formalised in the late 1930s, and Walter Winterbottom, first manager of the England football team and FA Director of Coaching, was an important figure in popularising it in England. This is one example of a coaching sheet produced by the FA that was distributed to schools. It shows how players learned specific skills.

Performance

Celtic manager Jock Stein talks to his
players in the bath after a match against
Tottenham Hotspur, 1967

Brooke Hendrix and Anna Moorhouse
recuperating in a recovery tub after training
with West Ham United, 2019

Scientific research has revolutionised
the way we think about rest, recovery and
rehabilitation. They are now seen as vitally
important for elite athletes, above all in
order to prevent injuries. Design is playing
a role in making these processes quicker,
easier and more enjoyable.

2

Identity

They Play
Roxanne Bottomley

Walking up Yorkshire Street, past The Royal Dyche pub, on a rainy day in April 2018. En route to Turf Moor stadium, every takeaway, taxi rank and pub is appropriately dressed in claret and blue. Burnley are playing Brighton & Hove Albion at home, and I arrive with imposter syndrome and a brand new Burnley shirt, aged twenty-five. It is an uneventful game with a 0-0 final score, yet to me it is the most exciting event I have ever attended.

●

I had never previously thought of myself as a sporty person, and at school football was not a sport that was even offered to girls. It was only when I was introduced to the game by an ex-partner, and surrounded by football talk at their family events, that I became interested in the world of sport. From my very first Burnley match I was hooked. I fell in love with the feeling of being part of something larger than myself, of being one person shouting in a sea of thousands, of having a shared identity. From this point on I had a dual identity: as a communication designer and researcher, but also a football player and fan.

Communication design plays a crucial role in providing greater access and inclusion across women's and queer football spaces. The way in which football is designed and who it is designed by are of great importance in the way we understand and feel connected to the sport. Why is it that I never saw women's football matches growing up? And if representation on television and social media had been more prominent when I was young, would I have been more likely to kick a ball around the park?

By profession I am a graphic design lecturer and researcher, and I am a queer intersectional feminist. To me this means applying queer notions of gender, sex and sexuality to the subject matter of intersectional feminism, a sociological framework through which various forms of inequality are explored and understood in relation to each other.[1] Questions around gender are rife in football, and becoming a football fan allowed me to consider the sport through this particular critical lens.

Football is highly gendered, and in the UK the sport is structurally biased towards cisgender men. Traditionally it is men who are the players, the fans and the people in control of the sport's institutions. This extends from club managers, coaches and referees through to commentators, broadcasters and governing bodies. Stereotypically masculine imagery and language has shaped the way the sport is viewed, and it is the male-dominated world of commercial football that forms the main visual narrative of the sport. Aspects of this narrative include war-like visual elements, showing masculine clichés of strength and power. Many football studies scholars have discussed the hyper-commodification of English football. This term speaks to the way in which English men's football, traditionally considered to be played with grit, for and by local working-class people with a sense of belonging, was transformed into a global business with predominantly commercial interests. This transformation was made possible with the introduction of digital broadcasting, which transmitted the men's English Premier League (EPL) around the world in the late twentieth and early twenty-first centuries. The breadth of professional and non-professional design within the men's game is vast, with many fans showing their support through crafting and making in a variety of modes and styles.

Women's Super League branding by Nomad, 2018

'This Girl Can' campaign by Sport England, launched in 2015

The range of visual material created by fans relating to the men's game is extensive, showing how the sport is experienced by many different people. However, the dominant visual narrative within the EPL remains that of battle-like commercially focused design displaying hyper-masculine tropes.

Women's football is also designed by a broad range of people, both professional and non-professional, and has a chance to change some of these stereotypes. 'From the shadows of the men's game to modern day superheroes': that is the vision for women's football.[2] The Women's Super League was rebranded in 2018 by the design studio Nomad. The rebrand followed a restructure of English women's football, which is now formed into three clear and distinct tiers: FA Women's Super League, FA Women's Championship and FA Women's National League. Hoping the rebrand would inspire the next generation of participants and spectators, Nomad involved players and fans of every age and level within their research and development stages. The women's game needed to be distinguishable from the men's English Premier League while being equally

appealing to a more diverse range of viewers. Emulating the men's game would not fit the brief, but nor would over-feminising the identity, as has often happened in the past. For the unofficial Women's World Cup hosted in Mexico in 1971, for example, a curvaceous mascot called 'Xochitl' was created, joined by a crew of similarly pouty cartoons to represent each of the participating nations.

Associating women in sport with power and strength has already been achieved through successful campaigns such as 'This Girl Can'. The campaign was developed by Sport England to get women and girls moving, regardless of shape, size or ability. It set a bar for inclusive sports campaigns that represent everyday women, with Nomad's challenge being to represent these characteristics in a way that felt authentic, specifically to the players and fans of women's football.

The first step in Nomad's rebrand was to create a series of icons to represent each of the league's tiers. These needed to fit together visually, but with each tier retaining its own unique characteristics. They were developed with the upward trajectory of the tier system in mind, suggesting how teams might work towards reaching their ultimate goal – the top of the league. At the top is the Women's Super League logo, which takes the form of a superhero's crest. Nomad drew the idea for this crest from the young players and fans they consulted, with women's football crowds typically including far more family groups than men's matches. Second in the tier system is the 'C' of the Women's Championship, a coiled spring shape that is meant to show its position as a place from which to bounce up into the Super League. Finally, the Women's National League consists of an 'N' made of many small intersecting forms. This represents the cooperative practices of the many clubs involved. The interlocking fragmented forms are a visual tool that ties the three tiers together, again depicting the way in which the tiers are individual but depend on each other to work as an integrated whole.

Following the rebrand, the opening weekend of the 2019/20 season saw a 1,137 per cent increase in attendance from the previous year. This increase in viewership of the Women's Super League has had a trickle-down effect, and grassroots women's football is

Football

more popular than ever. With an ever-growing number of teams popping up around the country, an equally large supply of DIY communication design has appeared, created by queer and women's football fans as well as the players.

The increase in popularity of inclusive grassroots football has meant a surge of creativity around the designing of badges, shirts, posters and other ephemera, many of which are created by non-professional designers. Having agency and authority over the way in which you communicate your club identity, politics and values is powerful. DIY communication design and self-authorship among communities of women and queer people means that the game is being designed from an alternative point of view to commercial cisgendered masculine football. This counter-narrative offers a queer feminist lens through which to view the sport.

Queerspace FC, an inclusive grassroots team based in Hackney Downs in East London, is an excellent example of such design. Queerspace are clear on their values and do not need external input to communicate this. Their logo and club badge are designed by teammates and partners Lili Donlon-Mansbridge and Katie Nelson. They use a simple visual metaphor for inclusion by overlapping the 2018 redesign of the Pride flag – which incorporates black and brown stripes representing people of colour, as well as pink, white and blue stripes from the Trans

Pride banner – with a line drawing of a football pitch. This can be seen as communication design in its purest form.

Other forms of communication design by non-professional designers are fanzines and fan-produced ephemera. Manchester United Women FC (MUWFC) is a relatively young club, as Manchester United only formed a women's team in 2018. Despite this short history, the community of fans supporting MUWFC is strong. The fan base have produced many banners that can be seen draped across the stands before games, and they have also started producing a fanzine, the *Barmy Article*, edited and organised by MUWFC fan Andy Slater. When talking about how the fans and creators of the fanzine made design decisions, Andy said they chose 'basically, red, black and white. Beyond that, it's all about the contributor. I don't want the mag to have any kind of agenda other than showcasing opinions, artwork and experiences of United Women fans.'[3]

The design of the fanzines is a truly collaborative effort by the fans and local community. Andy went on to say, 'The front covers of the first two issues were designed by different people, and other than the basic layout of the title and the preview of features, they were free to design whatever they wanted.' There is great freedom in designing and making for fun. Design powered by a love of football, and created without the prescriptive rules of a client or brief, frees up space for creativity and provides a platform for original fan-focused content. Andy stated, 'As we aren't professionals, I'm never too worried about perfection – my main aim is that it's engaging and easy to read.' The content and target audience are carefully considered and reflect the fact that many children attend the games. Andy explained that 'men's fanzines tend to be for adults only, but that wouldn't work in the women's game. It has to be family friendly and the puzzles at the back are aimed at kids.' At the time of writing the *Barmy Article* is on its third issue and is cherished by its community and supporters.

Fan-made design such as the work discussed above can be seen on social media pages, and at football games and tournaments, but very little of it is seen within institutions, nor has much of it been donated

Queerspace FC club badge

Dick, Kerr Ladies tour to Belgium, 1934

to museum archives. Therefore these designs, and their cultural significance, are at risk of being forgotten in years to come. The archiving of such material is important if we are to preserve the way football is communicated and experienced by women and queer players or fans. The National Football Museum (NFM) has an initiative to make its archive and museum collections material equally balanced between the men's and women's game. At the moment, the museum holds only a modest number of fan-made items for women's football, but this is something it is actively working to change. To help fill this gap, the rapid archiving of this material is a focus of the doctoral research I am conducting. As part of this, there will be opportunities for visitors to *Football: Designing the Beautiful Game*, the exhibition this book accompanies, to donate their designs to the National Football Museum archives. The rapid archiving will also take place at inclusive grassroots football tournaments where many player-made kits, stickers and other ephemera can be seen.

One of the main categories of items currently existing in the NFM archives, within women's football fandom, is historical scrapbooks. There is a long history of scrapbooking among football fans, and although this is generally something we associate with the men's game, there is also a rich culture of scrapbooking within women's football. The NFM archives have a selection of scrapbooks made by players and fans of the women's game, but this is only a small selection compared to the abundance of material assumed to be either lost or in the homes of women around the UK.

The earliest scrapbook documenting the women's game within the NFM archives dates back to the 1930s, and was made for Dick, Kerr Ladies. In 1917 Alfred Frankland, who was a manager at Dick, Kerr's Munitions Factory in Preston, suggested that the female employees should form a team after seeing them play during their lunch breaks. At the time this was fairly common, with women's factory teams popping up across the north of England throughout 1917. Dick, Kerr Ladies became one of the most famous teams in women's football history. The scrapbook documents Dick, Kerr Ladies' 1934 tour to Belgium. This scrapbook

Football

is of particular interest, as it documents the socialising that happens around a football tour. The page illustrated here shows three photographs in a symmetrical composition, with one image upright and central, and the other two either side of it at an angle. The maker used white marker or paint to form angular and linear graphic elements at the top corners of the page. The odd angles give the page a dynamic sense of playfulness, hinting at the fun the team were having on tour. There are a range of poses depicted in the three photographs. The one on the far left shows two football players looking confident in their kits. The photo seems to have been taken after a match, as the players have muddy knees. The two women are in a strong standing position with crossed arms. The players look burly, powerful and unconcerned with seeming feminine. The middle photograph depicts two women standing arm in arm, looking at one another with admiration. When the visual aspects of the scrapbook are viewed from a queer perspective, it could be suggested that the photos show women acting outside of the social norms for their presumed gender and sexuality. Not only are they playing football – considered a 'gentlemen's' sport – but their poses, clothing choice and attitude queer the way in which we see their gender and sexuality.

Another of the scrapbooks in the archive documents Corinthian Ladies' tour in Reims, France, in the 1970s. Corinthian Ladies was founded in 1949 by Percy Ashley, a scout for Bolton Wanderers and a local referee. Percy started the team mainly so that his daughter Doris could have somewhere to play football. The scrapbook is carefully crafted and compiled by Gladys Aiken, the mother of one of the team's players, Carol Aiken. Gladys took charge of the team in the 1960s, and her scrapbooks helped to show the intimate journey the team went on during this time. The splicing together of newspaper cuttings, postcards, drawings and travel documents provides an insider's view of a football team's tour of Reims. These scrapbooks offer important counter-narratives coming from players and fans rather than historians and journalists.

Further research into the culture of fan- and player-made design within the women's game will unlock these important histories and enrich our understanding of the game

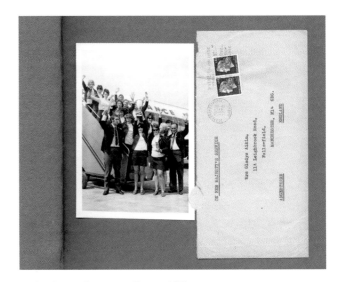

Corinthian Ladies tour to France, 1970s

overall, from diverse personal perspectives rather than commercially focused ones. The women's game has a bright future. We can see, through the designs discussed in this catalogue, the way in which women's football throughout history is represented in ways that counteract the hyper-masculine and hetero-normative view of the sport. Documenting and archiving the visual culture of women's football, particularly that made by fans and players, will ensure that women, young girls and queer folk control their own narrative within contemporary football.

I bring this writing to a close on a Sunday afternoon following a 6-1 defeat playing against Leeds Hyde Park FC Women. My legs are sore and marked with the imprint of the ball. As I catch my breath and thank the opposing team for a great game, I see a local children's mixed-gender team getting ready to take the pitch from us. A child of no more than ten years old is doing keepie-uppies, wearing a Lucy Bronze shirt. The face of the game is changing.

1   Mimi Marinucci, *Feminism is Queer* (London: Zed Books, 2016), p. 139.

2   Nomad Studio, www. nomadstudio.com/work/ fawomens [accessed 10 November 2021].

3   Andy Slater, personal communication, October 2021.

They Play

'If You Fillet a Fish, You Know How It's Made, Right?'
Floor Wesseling in conversation with Eleanor Watson

Eleanor Watson	Floor, can you tell us a little bit about how you got into kit design?
Floor Wesseling	It all started with my interest in heraldry. When I was a student at the [Gerrit] Rietveld Academie, my father gave me this book, which had belonged to my grandfather, that was an old manual on heraldry. I became really interested in it, because as a graphic designer you are mostly dealing with the question of identity – how to build a visual identity – and here was this visual language that was a thousand years old. I started using this as a sort of toolkit in my work, but it didn't result in anything serious until 2004, when I was in Portugal watching a football match with my friends. One of them announced that he was moving to Milan, and we had a big debate about which team he would support, AC or Inter. I thought, 'You know what, I'm going to buy him one shirt from each club and cut them up and sew them together.' The idea came to me because it is one of the chapters from the heraldry book, about a process called marshalling. When two noble families are joined through marriage, the offspring get a new crest that is half from the mother and half from the father. But then I thought that it could be more of a Romeo-and-Juliet approach, where the two families are not happily joined but rivals. And that was the start of my journey with kits. I was invited to create a lot of exhibitions, combining different shirts to tell the stories of cities, countries, local rivalries, etc. By cutting these shirts up, I learned a lot about how they are designed and manufactured. If you fillet a fish, you know how it's made, right?
EW	And this is when Nike brought you on board?
FW	Yes, Stuart McArthur, who is one of the creative directors at Nike, called me up and asked me to join the team after he saw my work. I asked him if it meant I could design the Dutch national kit and he said yes, so of course I had to join. For a few years it was me and two other guys designing all of the kits for the countries represented by Nike – Brazil, Holland, Portugal, Turkey, England (for a while), China ... I started working with professional players, designing shirts for people like Cristiano Ronaldo. My personal favourite was Wesley Sneijder, though. He was sample size, which helps, and he was very honest. I would present him with a shirt, and he would say, 'Yeah I love it, Floor, but I'm not going to wear it. I want a simple V-neck.' Because that is the least obstructive thing for a player to wear, so that is what they want.

If You Fillet a Fish

EW	Did you design the lettering as well as the shirts themselves?
FW	Yes, sometimes. For the 2014 FIFA World Cup I was able to do all of the design work for my top five teams, including the Dutch team of course. That was quite special, because I got to work with Wim Crouwel, a Dutch graphic designer who is one of my heroes. I went to him and asked if he liked football. He said no. I asked if he likes the colour orange. He said no. Then I asked if he would help me, and he said yes. It was great being able to be the student again, and to learn from him.
EW	Are there any special considerations you have to keep in mind when designing football typefaces?
FW	With the national teams especially, there are a lot of rules. There are the rules imposed by FIFA around the size of the lettering, the size of the crest, the placement of these things. Then there are the rules set by the sports brand, around the overall creative direction. The basic consideration though is whether it's legible, both on the pitch and on screen. It needs to be quite robust, so that it can withstand being condensed, can be bent and curved across the shoulders if the player has a long name. It's better to make something that isn't too square, especially for numbers, and not to go bonkers with too many outlines.
EW	The world of football typefaces seems to be a largely anonymous one, as brands don't tend to credit individual designers for their work. Were there any football designers whose work influenced your own?
FW	To be honest I wasn't familiar with any of them before I started at Nike. I looked at Neville Brody's work for the England team, but that was it – it's really such a niche world. I was very lucky that during my time at the Rietveld Academie I had an amazing typography teacher, the type god Gerard Unger. He taught me a lot. But with football type-faces it is quite different from other work, because you are not creating proper typefaces with a whole family and different weights and everything. You can go a little bit crazy, and consequently you see a lot of mistakes and some really stupid designs.
EW	Zooming out from lettering to look at the design of the kit overall, do you have any golden rules that you stick to in your work?

Football

Netherlands away kit, designed by Floor Wesseling, 2014

FW   Of course. The first is to understand and respect the difference between the home and away kits. The home kit should always read 'football'; it should read 'your club', 'your country'. You don't mess about with it. You can go sophisticated with the detail, design a nice neckline, detail on the cuffs, a lot of care and richness on the crest so that you get this sense of tailoring, and you make the person wearing the shirt feel proud. And then you can go mental with the away kit. The shirt I'm most proud of was the Dutch away kit for 2014. I almost lost my job fighting for that design, because it was very difficult to get the printing method right and everyone was running out of patience. I was told to drop it, and then – like a divine intervention – I bumped into the guys from the factory in China that was producing it just outside the elevator in my office in Amsterdam. They were visiting for something else but recognised me, so I got to talk to them, and they agreed to try some new methods on the sly. The result was amazing. I got to see the Dutch team wearing that kit in Brazil during their game against Spain. Because of the sublimation printing process that was used, some of the holes in the fabric closed up a bit and it affected the porosity of the fabric. When you put water on it, it starts to shine a bit. During the second half of the match it started raining, and the players got drenched and started to glow. We won 5-1.

If You Fillet a Fish

A View from the Pitch:

Now You Know We Exist
Trisha Lewis

Away from the eye-watering billions and the commercialisation of elite football is a thriving grassroots scene. Dotted across muddy parks, AstroTurf complexes and indoor pitches are clubs designed to provide all people with a safe place to play football, regardless of their ability. And Romance FC have been spearheading this movement for almost a decade.

Founded in East London in 2012 by Trisha Lewis, Romance FC initially formed from a group of friends who had met through the Boiler Room music scene. Their first sessions in Hackney's London Fields were chaotic but immediately successful, and the club has been transformative in bringing women and non-binary people together to play football, build community and create networks in the creative industries over the last decade. From organising international small-sided tournaments to curating panel discussions and innovative events, and from playing a key role in the official global launch film for FIFA 21 to collaborating with adidas and Pharrell Williams' Humanrace on a globally iconic football shirt, Trisha's work with the club has redefined what an amateur team can do through a strong visual identity, and a commitment to its roots.

●

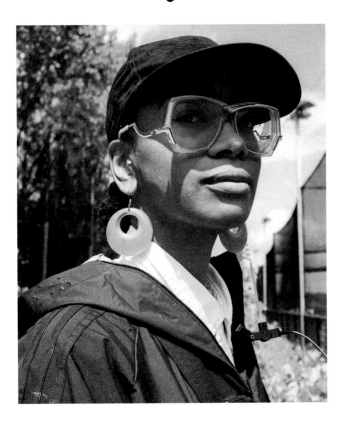

There was a sense of nervousness and excitement all bound into one in those initial sessions, but they were immensely refreshing. We were a group of adult women, mostly strangers, working in the creative industry, coming together to try something new ... and it soon became the thing I looked forward to the most. It felt very much like a family from the start.

In 2013, we had our first print feature in *i-D* magazine's 'Together' issue. We didn't have a kit, we weren't models, and it was the first time we'd ever had a proper team picture taken.

To see our image included in such a prestigious publication, captured at our previous divot-filled ground of Haggerston Park in London, totally blew us away. We weren't used to seeing collectives like ours spotlighted for just playing football, so it was a really special moment to know we were doing something quite admirable and that others could see themselves in us.

You're not only supporting us as a football team when wearing a shirt, you're supporting what we stand for: as marginalised communities, as individuals and as people who just want to be themselves freely and play without any discrimination. This is the standard we are setting at a grassroots level, and with more support, it can stretch a lot further.

For big brands to recognise the importance of the club and community is super humbling. We didn't start the team to gain any sort of accolade, so for these brands to take notice, listen to the needs of our community and work with us is massively significant in making actual change. There's only so much you can achieve when you are an outsider looking in, so in order to really understand a community you have to work with them, push the ego aside and share leadership.

To see other people, people who don't play for the team or aren't from London or don't know any of us personally, wearing the adidas x Humanrace FC shirt gives me a warm feeling of accomplishment. I'm starstruck from the perspective of 'Wow, you see us, you know we exist?' Seeing our shirt now being worn and celebrated all over the world is still a bit of a pinch-me moment, especially as we weren't even seen as a proper team at one point.

Trisha Lewis was interviewed by James Bird, photograph by Stephanie Sian Smith

A View from the Pitch

A View from the Pitch:

The Scouse Bayeux Tapestry
Peter Carney

Peter Carney tells stories through banners. You'll see them every time Liverpool play a match at home. As the players walk out onto the pitch and the whole ground reverberates with a lung-busting rendition of the club's anthem 'You'll Never Walk Alone', Anfield's iconic Spion Kop Stand becomes a bubbling patchwork of fabric design: more than 12,000 people in a roofed, single-tier, south-west-facing stand, each covered in different bits of material, each one telling a different story. Stories of Liverpool heritage and the importance of community. Stories of brilliant goals and social tragedies. Stories of political wrongdoing and European trophies. And many of them are made by Peter Carney.

It's no wonder that Peter's work on the Hillsborough memorial banner has been described as 'the Scouse Bayeux Tapestry'.

Since making his first banner in 1974 on the day of a Liverpool FA Cup semi-final replay that he couldn't attend, Peter has utilised techniques ranging from stencils to vinyl, Sellotape to hand stitching to tell these rich, intense and complex stories of Liverpool on and off the pitch. Here, he tells us why.

●

Liverpool thrives on the idea that 'it's the village that makes the child'. At any one point, everyone will be on their own, but we are always connected to others somehow, whether we like it or not. Family, friends, football. Scousers always come together, especially in hard times, to make things better for the city. Don't get me wrong, that can be really hard at times, but football is the prime example of people pulling together for one aim.

It's the faith I had in something Bill Shankly said about Liverpool, particularly a speech following the 1971 FA Cup final defeat ('I have told my players that they are priv-ileged to play for you'), that kept me going after Hillsborough. I really do believe that there's a sense of community in Liverpool like nothing else in this country: a sense of belong-ing, support, togetherness.

I try to tell that tale through my banners. The new Hillsborough memorial banner, for instance, is a community banner. Technically, I'm trying to reach all the senses of your being. It's a touching banner, emotionally

Peter Carney, *More banner*, 2007

and literally. For me, that's an existential thing from being in Pen 3 at Hillsborough and getting carried out unconscious. I'm trying to bring all the senses I regained to the banner. The colours are strong and vibrant, so anyone with impaired vision can have a chance of picking it up. The sense of touch is there, the names are embroidered and stand proud. There are different cloths to project different things: rough for Hillsborough, satin for the trophy flames, the Liver bird and headline script: We Never Walk Alone.

I met a fella, Mick Brennan, at an event recently to help people with dementia. Turned out he lived around the back of where I live. I saw him out walking one day, said how are ya and that, and he told me he had a load of old souvenirs and newspapers to give away as he was moving house. Turns out, this guy sits close to me at the game. In among the newspapers Mick gave me are the inquest testimonies from the families of people killed at Hillsborough. I've wanted for a while to put a QR code on the banner to link to a website that speaks the stories of those who were killed. This guy has given me the means to do that, so that will complete all of the senses. It has flowers on it too, for the sense of smell, and representing those in our community who created the magnificent field of flowers.

I try to encourage others to be part, to take part, to say and have their say in the stories of Liverpool; to be involved and see themselves reflected in what I do. That reflection and echo is then what everyone else sees of us.

Peter Carney was interviewed by James Bird

A View from the Pitch

Scottish international badge, 1877

Football badges were first worn at the first international match in 1872, a goalless game between England and Scotland. England adopted the three lions as its crest, a symbol that dates to the reign of King Richard I, who used it for his Royal Seal of 1198. The Scottish team wore a badge showing the lion rampant, a symbol from the Royal Banner of Scotland that has symbolised the Kingdom of Scotland since 1222.

Football

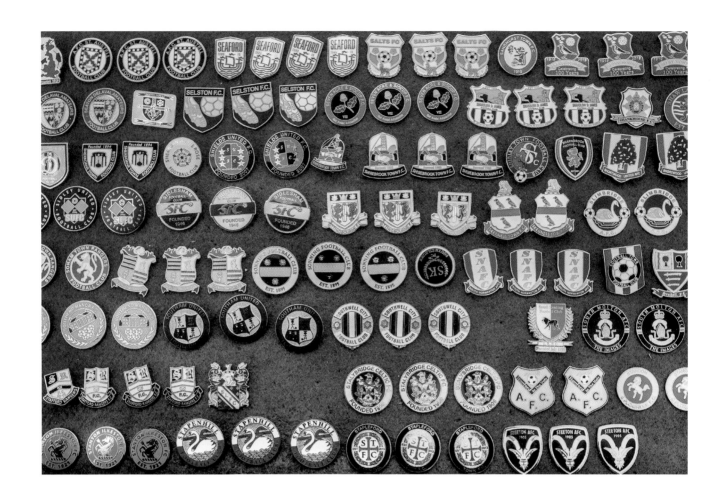

Pin badges, c.1980–2000

In the late 1800s, crests became more elaborate as clubs sought to establish their credibility and reputation. Many assumed their town or city coat of arms, creating a sense of history and belonging. Local industry and buildings were also common sources of inspiration, and they continue to act as symbols for clubs today, even when the landmarks no longer exist.

Identity

SCOTTISH

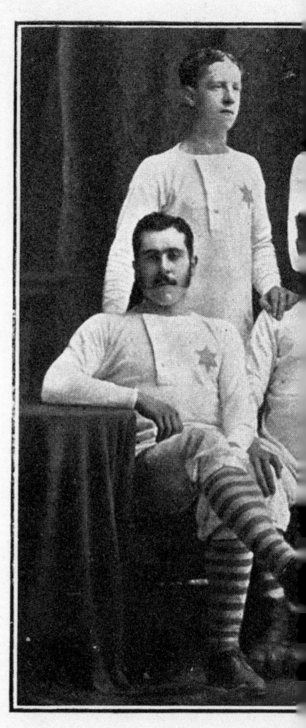

Back Row—George

Middle Row—William Dur

Front

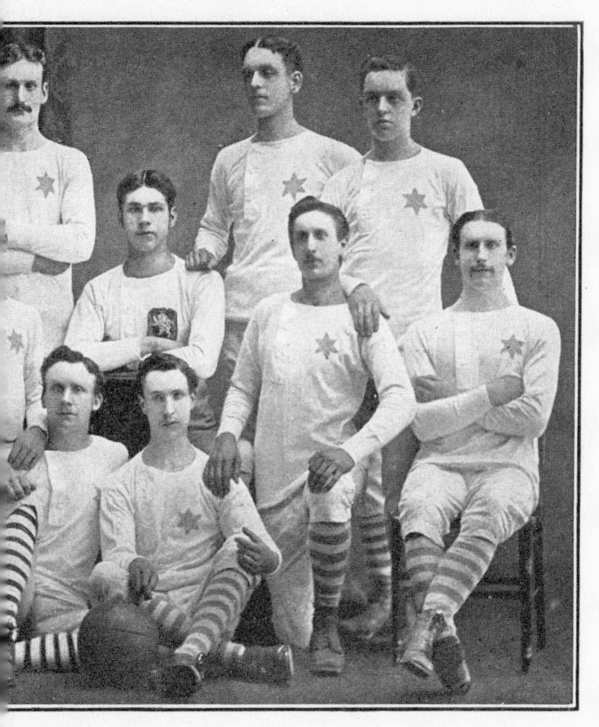

ie, William M'Neil, Tom Vallance, and J. M. Watt.

David Hill, Peter Campbell, Moses M'Neil, and Sam Ricketts.

James A. K. Watson and A. Marshall.

See page 19.

Development of Juventus' logo,
1905—2020

Football

Selection of crests from members
of the Confederation of Independent
Football Associations (CONIFA)

Crests can be an important means
of expression for marginalised
groups. CONIFA, the Confederation
of Independent Football Associations,
represents unofficial states that are
not permitted to compete in the FIFA
World Cup. It supports international
football teams from unrecognised
nations, regions, minority groups and
isolated territories, allowing them to
meet and compete against each other.
CONIFA currently has sixty members,
including Sápmi, Tibet and Abkhazia.

Identity

Football

Olive, *GIRLFANS*, Issue 1, Anfield,
Alex Hurst, 2013

GIRLFANS is an ongoing photography
project that aims to capture the female
fan experience and give more visibility
to female football supporters. Created
by Jacqui McAssey in 2013, the project
includes five distinct portrait series,
each capturing the fans of a different
UK club. Portraits are distributed in a
traditional football fanzine format.

BELOW

Protests outside Hull City ground, 2018

The redesign of crests can cause
controversy. In recent years, many clubs
have been acquired by investors without
cultural ties to the club or its community.
These investors often seek to adapt
the crest to make it more appealing to
international audiences. These changes
can be seen as tangible evidence of
money taking precedence over heritage
and are often bitterly disputed.

Identity

Women's football socks, caps and belt,
c. 1895

Football

Pitt Street Revue v. Portsmouth Ladies
1916

Identity

Harrow Footers team, 1871

Football

Identity

APPROVED COLOURS
FOR GOALKEEPERS' JERSEYS

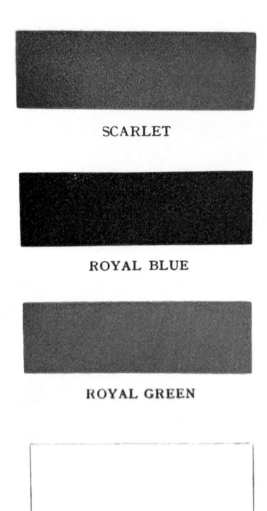

SCARLET

ROYAL BLUE

ROYAL GREEN

WHITE

'Approved colours for goalkeepers' jerseys', extract from the Football Association rulebook, c.1920

All players in a football team wear the same kit apart from the goalkeeper. Goalies are the only players allowed to touch the ball with their hands, so they need to be easily distinguished from other players. Until the 1970s, UK goalkeepers were only allowed to play in green, blue, scarlet or white for domestic games. Green was preferred, as few teams wore this colour as their main kit.

Child's mascot shirt, Sheffield
Wednesday, 1960s

Mascots are another important
football symbol. They act as a playful
representation of the team and are
thought to bring good luck. Mascots
are often based on a team's nickname
and can take the form of an animal or
a fictional local personality.

Identity

Pelé at the 1966 FIFA World Cup™

For international matches, kit colours
are chosen to communicate a team's
national identity. The most famous kit
is the yellow of the Brazilian national
team. A symbol of flair, innate talent and
creativity, the Brazilian national kit has
been worn by some of football's greatest
players. It was worn by Pelé during the
1958 FIFA World Cup, when he was just
17 years old. He scored two of Brazil's
five goals against Sweden in the final,
marking the beginning of his career
as an international footballing star.

Football

Original sketches for a new Brazil
national kit, Aldyr Garcia Schlee, 1953

In 1950, Brazil suffered a humiliating loss
to Uruguay in the FIFA World Cup final
while wearing their traditional all-white
kit. It was subsequently deemed unlucky,
and a national competition was launched
to find a replacement colour. The winner
of the competition was 18-year-old
newspaper illustrator Aldyr Garcia
Schlee. Living in a small community
on the Uruguayan–Brazilian border,
Schlee was intrigued by the competition's
only stipulation: that the kit include all
four colours of the Brazilian national
flag. Most kits include a maximum of
three colours, and he had to rise to the
challenge of creating a harmonious
design that met this criterion.

Identity

Umbrochure, 1950/51, 1950

Many kit designs have basic templates. These range from simple stripes, sashes or quarters to more complex patterns and detailing. Clubs simply need to choose a template and add their own colours to create a bespoke design. Manchester kit manufacturer Umbro was an early champion of templates, offering a variety of designs in their *Umbrochure* since 1935.

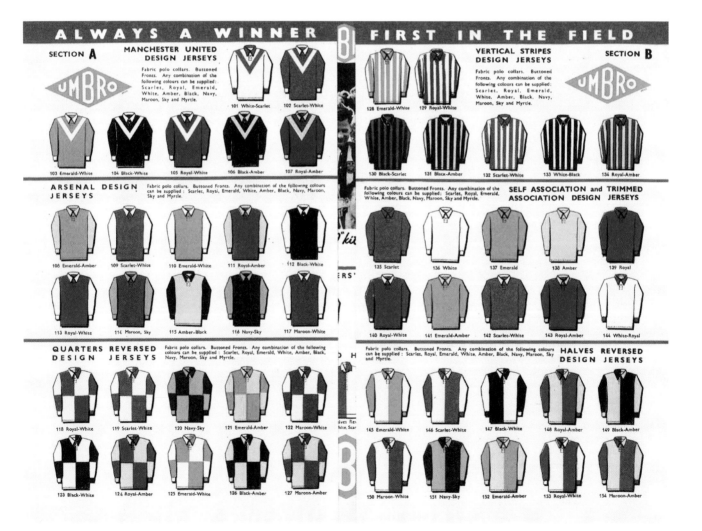

Football

Dick, Kerr Ladies football team, 1920s

Early pattern designs were limited by the manufacturing options available, as it was not possible to weave or print complex designs. This led to several clubs wearing the same kit, as with the bold black and white stripes of Notts County and Newcastle United, now commonly associated with Italian team Juventus. Today, stripes are worn by more than 160 league teams worldwide and were once the kit for the pioneering women's team Dick, Kerr Ladies, named after the factory for which they worked.

Identity

Football

Arsenal take part in numbered shirts experiment, 1933

It is difficult to say which team was the first to wear kit numbers, but an early example came in 1933 when both Chelsea and Arsenal wore numbers for their opening Football League matches. The experiment was welcomed by the press because it allowed 'spectators to give credit for each bit of good work to the correct individual'. Despite this, the use of numbers was not adopted by the Football Association until 1939.

Identity

Michelle Akers during a group
match between Brazil and USA,
FIFA Women's World Cup™ 1991,
in Panyu, Guangzhou, China

The number 10 is traditionally worn
by a team's primary playmaker or an
attacking midfielder. Playing between
the midfield and the forward line, the
number 10 makes links across the
field of play and creates chances for
their teammates. Some of the greatest
players in the history of the game
have worn the number 10, giving it a
prestige that few other numbers have.

Football

Michel Platini, match-worn France shirt, adidas, 1984

Lionel Messi, Argentina shirt prepared for 2014 FIFA World Cup™, adidas, 2014

Zico, match-worn Brazil shirt from 1986 FIFA World Cup™, Topper, 1986

Diego Maradona, match-worn Argentina shirt from 1979 international friendly, adidas, 1979

Identity

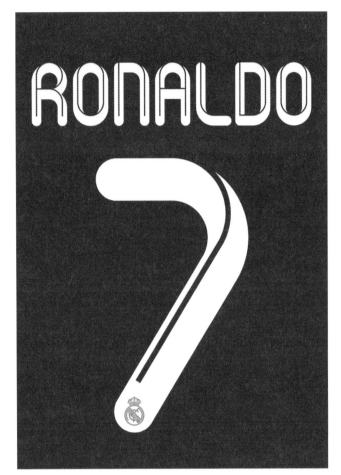

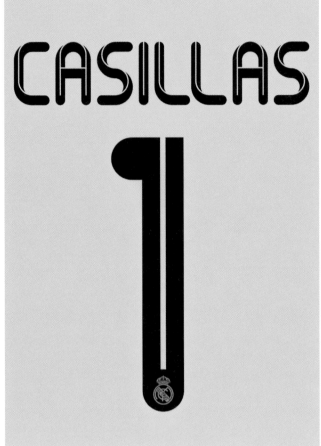

Real Madrid typeface, 2011–12
Anthony Barnett for Sporting iD, 2011

Anthony Barnett designed a huge
number of typefaces during his career
in football graphics, producing work
for Real Madrid, Liverpool, Manchester
United and Fenerbahçe, among others.
Though his work is immediately
recognisable to many, he remains
largely unknown as a designer, because
sportswear manufacturers do not
typically credit individual designers
for their work.

2010 Africa Cup of Nations typeface, preparatory sketches, Paul Barnes for Puma, 2010

Paul Barnes is a British designer and typographer responsible for producing some of the most recognisable typefaces in football. Alongside work for the English and Italian national teams, Barnes was commissioned by sportswear brand Puma to produce a shirt typeface for the 2010 Africa Cup of Nations. Inspired by the irregular and characterful hand-painted signs found across the African continent, the typeface was worn on the shirts of Algeria, Cameroon, Côte d'Ivoire and Ghana.

Identity

Ian Wright, Arsenal v. Bolton Wanderers,
Mark Leech, 1997

English player Ian Wright, a prolific
goalscorer for Arsenal, marked the
moment he broke his club's all-time
record with this vest reveal. It plays
on the strapline used in sports brand
Nike's advertising.

 Until banned by FIFA in 2014, it
was customary for footballers to wear
personalised shirts underneath their
team kit. These were often revealed
to share messages such as tributes
to family, friends or supporters, or
broader social and political statements.
A variation on this custom came in
1999 when Brandi Chastain ripped off
her shirt to reveal her sports bra after
scoring the winning penalty for the US
national team in the FIFA Women's World
Cup final. The image became a symbol
of confident female athleticism and a
rallying cry for women's participation
in football.

Football

Brandi Chastain revealing her sports bra,
USA v. China, Roberto Schmidt, 1999

Identity

Advertisement for 'Umbroset for Boys'
Umbro, late 1970s

Football shirts made for fans are known
as replica kits. The replica kit industry
was initially targeted at children, with
Umbro releasing the 'Umbroset for
Boys' in 1959. It was the first time that
manufacturers actively promoted
kits for individuals rather than teams.
Although they have become a billion-
pound industry, replica kits for adults
only became popular in the late 1980s.
They are made from lower-grade fabrics
than the kits worn by players, and
sometimes have smaller numbers and
typefaces to further distinguish them
from the team shirts.

Football

Leeds United under Don Revie were the
first team to sign a shirt sponsorship
deal, with Admiral. They are shown here
with the Football League Championship
trophy, 1 August 1974

Identity

Romance FC kit, Pharrell Williams x
adidas, 2020

Football

Fiorentina home kit, 1998/99, FILA, 1998

Following the introduction of
manufacturers' logos on shirts, clubs
soon began including those of other
sponsors. In 1979, Liverpool was the first
English team to carry a shirt sponsor,
the Japanese conglomerate Hitachi,
with many other clubs following suit.
Today, the sponsor's logo has become
a standard element of kit design, with
certain logos even gaining cult status.

Identity

Champions League Koulikoro
Émile-Samory Fofana
2018–20

This series of portraits by Franco-Malian photographer Émile-Samory Fofana captures the global influence of major football leagues by documenting the worldwide prevalence of replica kits. In the photographer's words, 'When the jersey of an Argentinian midfielder, playing in the British Premier League, in a club sponsored by a United Arab Emirates airline, designed by an American kit supplier and produced in China, is worn by an 11-year-old boy in Mali, it becomes a matter of geopolitics. Football mirrors the world's patterns.'

Identity

Palmeiras 1990 home shirt

Newcastle 1995 home shirt

TOP ROW
Netherlands 1988 home shirt

BOTTOM ROW
Cameroon 2002 home shirt

Identity

Denmark 1986 home shirt

Arsenal 1991 away shirt

Football

TOP ROW
Parma 1997 home shirt

BOTTOM ROW
England 1996 goalkeeper's shirt

Identity

121

Group of 'casuals', 1980s

Football fans sometimes create their own uniforms beyond replica kits. An example of this is the 'casuals' of the late 1970s and 80s, a British subcultural movement that saw young fans dress in luxury European sportswear. The look allowed fans to express and share an identity, making clothing an important part of football culture. Items were sourced while fans travelled to Europe to watch their teams play in away games, with popular brands including adidas, Sergio Tacchini, Fila and Diadora.

Football

JOE WAG GOES TO HOLLAND

JOE WAG Part 2.

In issue No.3 of "The End" we saw how our hero went shopping in London, and after telling his mates about his exploits Joe convinced them that a trip to the continent would be even better.

Joe Goes to Europe

Joe and a few of his cronies had decided on a trip to Holland, which quite by chance coincided with a certain pre-season football tour. The intention of this trip was purely to take in the sights as any other tourist would do. But also on the list of attractions were certain sports shops and jewelry stores (these had always fascinated Joe, but he could never explain why).

Joe and his mates purchased return train tickets to Amsterdam and with holdall in hand, set off on a warm August morning. (Joe was not going to waste time trying to bunk, when more important things were at stake). The channel crossing was pretty uneventful and the contingent was content to "get their heads down." Just before they docked Joe spotted a film star, namely "Dikey" from the "Going Out" series (one of Joe's idols). Joe felt that he and Dikey had alot in common, both had been brought up in working class homes, both had been rebels, and both had won through in their own way, Dikey was a star, and Joe was notorious in other ways.

After slipping through customs the lads made their way up to Amsterdam and booked into a Hotel which was situated in the "red light" area of the city. That night the lads went out for a drink, and met up with a group of lads who were also from the "promised land" and a great time was had by all. Joe, wherever he went in Europe, always bumped into someone he knew, or someone he had heard of on the scallies grapevine, and this always made Joe feel happy, so happy that he invited everyone back to the Hotel de Cesspit. An all night session went on that very night, with old borstal stories, jokes and rowdy football songs being the order of the day. Joe was interested in the other lads stories, as they had at one time or another been housed in one of Her Majesty's establishments, unlike Joe who was never caught, he had in the past been likened to the Scarlet Pimpernel.

Next day the lads left the Hotel by way of the back window (no explanation was ever given for this) and made heir way to the city centre. After looking around for a while, Joe and his co-horts entered a jewellers store and were astonished to see a tray of sovereigns on the counter with no shop assistant in sight. Before they realized it they were out of the door and moving briskly away. Booking into a different hotel they then decided to go to the football match between a combined Merseyside XI and Ajax.

Going to the game was to be Joe's downfall as he found himself in the middle of a fracas between rival fans. Although as you may have guessed Joe was quite innocent, he was pulled in, while members of the "lunatic fringe" got away scot free. In the struggle to the local station, Joe's brand new cord jacket which he had acquired while "shopping" in Amsterdam was unfortunately torn. This really upset Joe, but worse was to come, and a search of his hotel room by the police recovered the rings. Joe appeared in court and was given a custodial sentence, after which he was deported back home, where he was able to relax and plan further excursions to the continent. Anyone wishing to hear Joe's tale of woe can contact him at Renshaw Hall Box 36 11.15 Wednesday morning. Next issue Joe goes to Paris.

Ten Easy Lessons How to be a Scouser by Joe Wag

1. Buy "The End" and burn your birmo's and star jumpers.
2. Buy a pair of training shoes. Preferably Adidas, Puma or Nike. Throw out your stack-heels or brown air-wear.
3. Buy a pair of faded jeans and green anorak.
4. Get the jeans taken in by Chris Davies Alterations.
5. Buy a baggy jumper or wear one of your dads.
6. Start making expressions up or listen to other expressions and learn them off by heart. eg., "Get your head together," "I'm shot to bits," "I'm totally done in," "That's sad" etc. The important thing is that no-one else understands them.
7. Get a membership for Ratsby's, and a menu from the Fung Loy.
8. Start going to the match and getting your face seen, especially before away matches at Lime Street and in London Tube Stations.
9. Buy all "The Jam's" L.Ps.
10. Appear apathetic about everything except for action, and get good at pool. Also shorten words and put 'O' on the end.

Important:

Try to disguise that you've had a priviledged background, were educated at a Grammar school, you've got two cars and three tele's, and you go on holiday four times a year. NB. Pretend you are on the dole and have been to Risley, and you were born on Scottie.

JOE WAG (left) + YOUNG BROTHER (right)

6

Illustration from *The End*
Peter Hooton, 1982

'Casuals' culture was well documented in Liverpool-based fanzine *The End*. Co-founder Peter Hooton (lead vocalist for Liverpool band The Farm) was inspired by other satirical anarchist zines of the early 1980s. Running from 1981 to 1988, *The End* featured political cartoons and observational humour, as well as interviews with prominent musicians such as The Clash and The Undertones.

Two young Chelsea fans at the
FA Cup final, Chelsea v. Leeds United,
11 April 1970

Football

From the 1880s until the 1900s, match-day programmes and season handbooks were often single sheets. In the 1910s, the modern booklet with attractive covers emerged, with some of the finest designs coming from Chelsea, Arsenal and Aston Villa. Paper shortages during the First and Second World Wars signalled a return to simpler designs, until the late 1950s when programmes became more substantial and varied.

TOP ROW

Bolton Wanderers programme, 1966; Arsenal programme, 1939/40; Doncaster Rovers programme, 1962

BOTTOM ROW

Millwall programme, 1964; Doncaster Rovers handbook, 1962–3; Wolverhampton Wanderers programme, 1968

Football

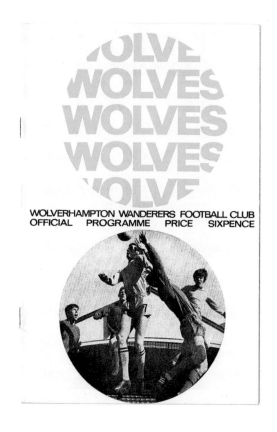

Identity

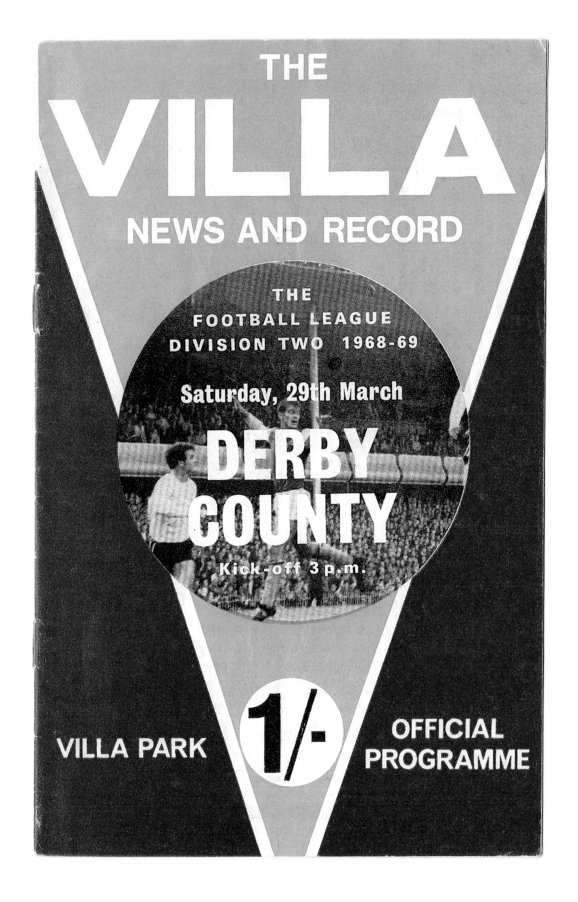

Identity

Football

Sky Blue match-day programme and process material, John Elvin, 1970/71

The 1970s are often considered to be a golden era for match-day programme design. Programmes became more substantial and featured playful layouts and bold experiments in typography. British designer John Elvin's work for Coventry City's *Sky Blue* match-day programme is emblematic of this shift in approach. Elvin turned *Sky Blue* into a fully fledged magazine that fans kept as a memento. His unique style of bold typography and high-contrast imagery earned a prize at the Design & Art Direction Awards in 1972. Elvin's style inspired the design of the endpapers for this catalogue.

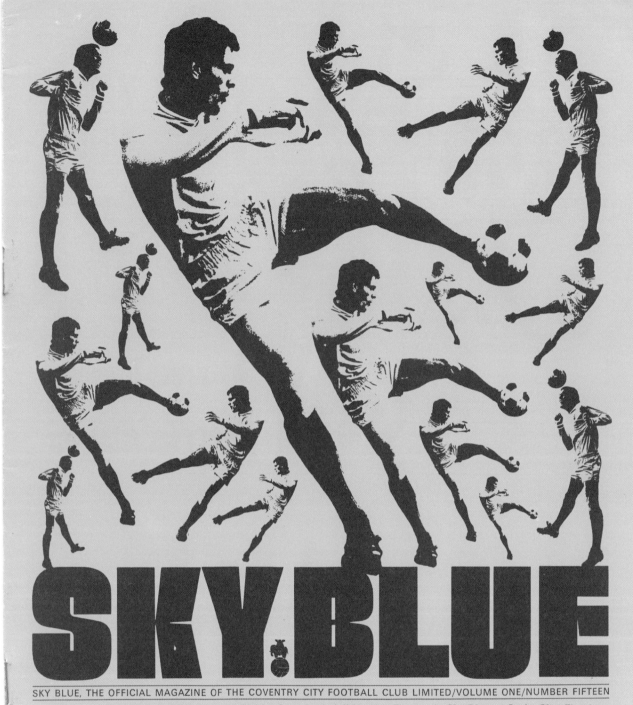

SKY.BLUE

SKY BLUE, THE OFFICIAL MAGAZINE OF THE COVENTRY CITY FOOTBALL CLUB LIMITED/VOLUME ONE/NUMBER FIFTEEN

Your 'Sky Blue' host for today's Football League Division One game is Jeff Blockley. The match : **Sky Blues v Stoke City.** The place : Highfield Road. The date : 5th December 1970. Kick-off : 3.15 pm. Goalkeeper Gordon Banks, captain of today's visitors in the absence of the injured Peter Dobing, brings to Highfield Road a Stoke side including some of the games most promising youngsters, Denis Smith, Terry Conroy, Mike Bernard and John Mahoney ! In today's magazine : Stoke, Focus on Jeff Blockley, Saturday Men and Junior Sky Blues.

PRESIDENT Dr CUTHBERT K. N. BARDSLEY, C.B.E., M.A. (LORD BISHOP OF COVENTRY). CHAIRMAN DERRICK H. ROBINS VICE-CHAIRMAN J. R. MEAD, J.P., F.C.A. DIRECTORS PETER D. H. ROBINS, MICHAEL FRENCH, F.C.A., THOMAS SERGEANT, F.R.C.S MEDICAL OFFICER Dr T. BAIRD. GENERAL MANAGER NOEL CANTWELL. SECRETARY EDDIE PLUMLEY, CHEF & CATERING MANAGER FRANK HUNT. MAITRE d'HOTEL GIOVANNI. ADVERTISING CONSULTANT PETER STURTZ. MAGAZINE EDITOR JOHN ELVIN

COVENTRY CITY v STOKE CITY/5th DECEMBER 1970/'SKY BLUE' OFFICIAL MATCHDAY MAGAZINE **2**/ (10 N.P.)

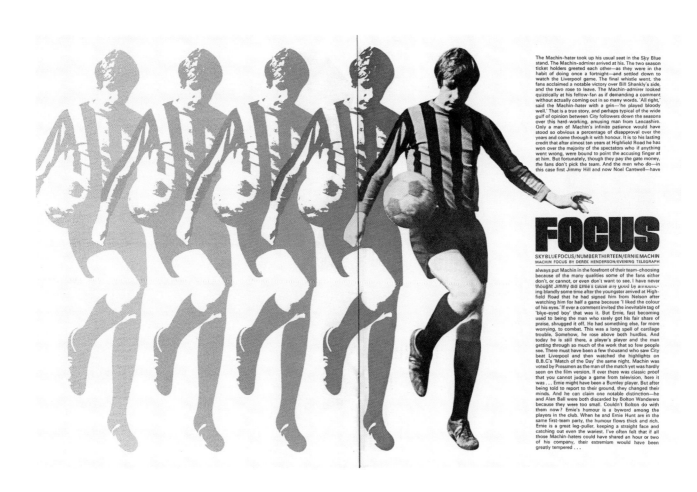

The Machin-hater took up his usual seat in the Sky Blue stand. The Machin-admirer arrived at his. The two season ticket holders greeted each other—as they were in the habit of doing once a fortnight—and settled down to watch the Liverpool game. The final whistle went, the fans acclaimed a notable victory over Bill Shankly's side, and the two rose to leave. The Machin-admirer looked quizzically at his fellow-fan as if demanding a comment without actually coming out in so many words. 'All right,' said the Machin-hater with a grin—'he played bloody well.' That is a true story, and perhaps typical of the wide gulf of opinion between City followers down the seasons over this hard-working, amusing man from Lancashire. Only a man of Machin's infinite patience would have stood so obvious a percentage of disapproval over the years and come through it with honour. It is to his lasting credit that after almost ten years at Highfield Road he has won over the majority of the spectators who if anything went wrong, were bound to point the accusing finger at at him. But fortunately, though they pay the gate money, the fans don't pick the team. And the men who do—in this case first Jimmy Hill and now Noel Cantwell—have

FOCUS

SKY BLUE FOCUS/NUMBER THIRTEEN/ERNIE MACHIN
MACHIN FOCUS BY DEREK HENDERSON/EVENING TELEGRAPH

always put Machin in the forefront of their team-choosing because of the many qualities some of the fans either don't, or cannot, or even don't want to see. I have never thought Jimmy did Ernie's cause any good by announcing blandly some time after the youngster arrived at High-field Road that he had signed him from Nelson after watching him for half a game because 'I liked the colour of his eyes.' If ever a comment invited the inevitable tag of 'blue-eyed boy' that was it. But Ernie, fast becoming used to being the man who rarely got his fair share of praise, shrugged it off. He had something else, far more worrying, to combat. This was a long spell of cartilage trouble. Somehow, he rose above both hurdles. And today he is still there, a player's player and the man getting through so much of the work that so few people see. There must have been a few thousand who saw City beat Liverpool and then watched the highlights on B.B.C.'s 'Match of the Day' the same night. Machin was voted by Pressmen as the man of the match yet was hardly seen on the film version. If ever there was classic proof that you cannot judge a game from television, here it was . . . Ernie might have been a Burnley player. But after being told to report to their ground, they changed their minds. And he can claim one notable distinction—he and Alan Ball were both discarded by Bolton Wanderers because they were too small. Couldn't Bolton do with them now? Ernie's humour is a byword among the players in the club. When he and Ernie Hunt are in the same first-team party, the humour flows thick and rich. Ernie is a great leg-puller, keeping a straight face and catching out even the wariest. I've often felt that if all those Machin-haters could have shared an hour or two of his company, their extremism would have been greatly tempered . . .

Soften Up Hard Lad, Corbin Shaw, 2019

We Should Talk about Our Feelings,
Corbin Shaw, 2022

Corbin Shaw is a multidisciplinary
artist who uses the medium of football
banners to question traditional ideas
of masculinity and identity. Originally
from Sheffield, Shaw was impelled
by the suicide of a family friend.
By manipulating the familiar visual
language of football banners, Shaw
effectively comments on the importance
of mental health to football fans.

Destiny Delivered, Peter Carney and
Carmel Gittens, 2005, 2007

OPPOSITE

We Never Walk Alone, Peter Carney
and Christine Waygood, 2009, based
on original from 1989

Liverpool supporter Peter Carney
makes banners for the famous Kop end
at Anfield, a section of the terraces
reserved for home supporters. Alongside
designs celebrating players, coaches
and famous victories, some of Carney's
most significant work commemorates the
Hillsborough stadium disaster. In 1989,
Liverpool visited Sheffield Wednesday's
ground for an FA Cup semi-final, and
ninety-seven fans were killed in a human
crush. Carney survived and went on to
become a key campaigner in the fans'
fight for justice. His two memorial banners
– the first created in the week after the
tragedy and the second on its twentieth
anniversary – stand as a lasting tribute
to those whose lives were taken.

Football

Identity

Vera Hutchinson from *In Soccer Wonderland*, Julian Germain, 1990

In Soccer Wonderland draws together a range of images that reflect British photographer Julian Germain's perception of football, and what it means to him and other fans. Vera Hutchinson is the widow of a dedicated Sunderland fan, Harry Hutchinson, who never missed a match in over forty years. She is depicted in their garden, where the team's colours red and white cover every possible surface.

Football

Handmade supporter's scarf, Preston
North End, 1964

Before replica kits became available,
fans showed their support by wearing
hand-knitted scarves in their team
colours. The practice originated in the
UK, where these handmade items served
the dual purpose of allowing fans to
show their support while also keeping
them warm. Today scarves are worn
by fans across the world and are an
important element in crowd displays.

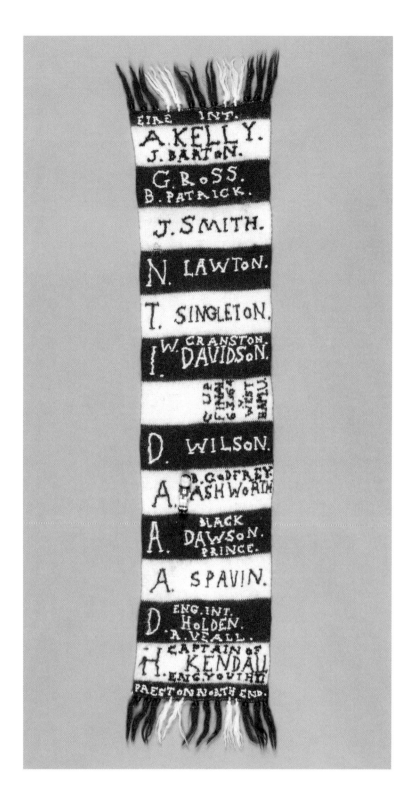

Identity

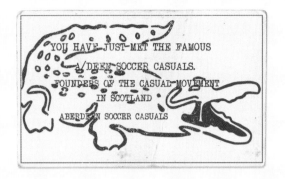

YOU HAVE JUST MET THE FAMOUS
A'DEEN SOCCER CASUALS.
FOUNDERS OF THE CASUAL MOVEMENT
IN SCOTLAND .
ABERDEEN SOCCER CASUALS

ON THE FIRST DAY GOD CREATED

6.57 CREW

DAY WE TOOK OVER DAY WE TOOK OVER.
PORTSMOUTH F.C

D.L.F.

DERBY   LUNATIC   FRINGE

'The Deterrent'

On Hire from Her Majesty's Service
via the Baseball Ground Asylum...

NOTTINGHAM FOREST
Executive Crew
away on business
THE MIDLANDS No.1

Hooligan calling cards

At the height of the football hooligan
era of the 1970s and 80s, rival gangs of
supporters or 'firms' would meet to fight
on the day of a match. These calling
cards, originally pioneered by West Ham's
Inter City Firm, were dropped at the scene
of a brawl to signify the victors' success.
The cards were designed by members of
the firm and often parodied the visual
language of British establishments.

Identity

TOP

Leyton Orientear, November 1987

BOTTOM

When Sunday Comes, October 1988

OPPOSITE

The End, 1982

Fanzines are unofficial publications created by a club's supporters that offer an alternative look at their team. The first football fanzine published in the UK was *Foul*, a sideways look at the state of football produced by University of Cambridge students between 1972 and 1976. *Foul* inspired a glut of fanzines in the 1980s, with prominent titles such as *When Saturday Comes* and Leeds United's *The Square Ball* still produced today. Taking inspiration from the anarchist zine movement of the 1970s, many fanzines have a political element: taking satirical aim at club policy as well as looking at on-field action.

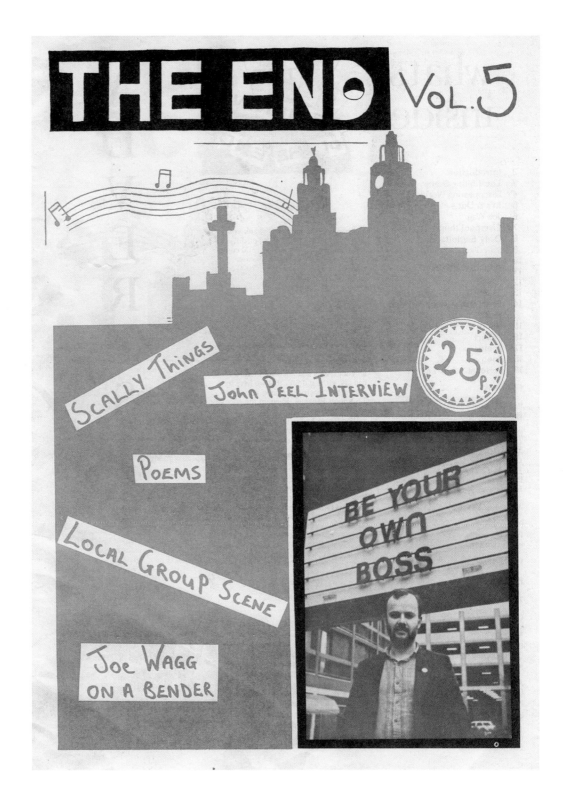

Venables stays cool

Chelsea Independent, September 1989

3

Crowds

Football Without Fans Is Nothing
Jacqui McAssey

Celtic manager Jock Stein famously said that 'Football without fans is nothing', and the coronavirus lockdowns of 2020 and 2021 confirmed this: football without fans is incredibly dull. An artificial crowd noise echoing around an empty stadium does not make for the pulsating spectacle that has captivated crowds for over a century. Originally places where men would socialise with each other and enjoy rivalries with teams from nearby towns, football crowds of the past were exposed to the elements in muddy paddocks and uncovered cowsheds. As football's popularity grew and grounds developed, swaying football terraces were mainly the preserve of working-class men, and in this environment the emotional bond between the stadium, team and fans was formed.

It does, however, seem fitting that in the fifty-first year of the lifting of the Football Association's ban on women's football, we might contemplate an alternative narrative in football, had women been allowed to play. Their continued involvement with the game, as players, spectators or policymakers, would surely have changed the hyper-masculine world of football. In the early days, Preston was a hotspot for women's football, with the famous Dick, Kerr Ladies being formed there

in 1894. On Boxing Day 1920, its match against St Helen's Ladies drew a crowd of more than 50,000, with thousands more who reportedly could not get into Goodison Park. Yet one year later, banned from using FA pitches, women were consigned to play in parks for the next half-century. Or consider the hidden history of the 'Lost Lionesses', the unauthorised England team who played at Mexico's Estadio Azteca at the unofficial World Cup in 1971. Some were as young as fourteen, and they talked of their disbelief at the sight and sound of up to 100,000 men, women and children welcoming them on to the pitch. Unknown at home but stars in Mexico – this was an inspirational

The Lost Lionesses, 1971 – England's team at the unofficial Women's World Cup

story and another opportunity missed in the promotion of football to women, and especially girls. The team returned home without fanfare or recognition.[1]

Female fans have been subjected to gender inequality directly and indirectly for as long as they've attended football matches. In 2021, the 'Women at the Match' report by the Football Supporters' Association stated that in addition to sexist comments and chants, an alarming one in five of the women surveyed had been subjected to unwanted physical attention at the match – double the number reported in the comparative report in 2014.[2] Female fans must repeatedly protect their space and prove their worth, or – as podcasters the Anfield Wrap put it in their 2018 'Women in Football' special – women are 'dealing with groping or harassment in pubs, and having to display football knowledge as a form of self-defence';in other words, being physically assaulted and quizzed at every turn.[3] These examples of sexism are exhausting.

The lack of information on women's experiences in football has also occurred in academia, where research has tended to focus on tribalism and hooliganism associated with male supporters. Recent studies however have made a significant contribution to our understanding of the changes in women's lives that have positively impacted female football fandom in the West. Primarily, in the 1960s the introduction of birth control – and with that, greater economic freedom – allowed women to steer their leisure activities and become fans of sport.[4]

Today, a number of fan-run initiatives exist which aim to reclaim space in footballing crowds for women to enjoy the game. Armed with information and a camera, but unlike the earlier, more polemic zines of the 1980s, GIRLFANS fanzine began in 2013 as a study of female football fans, and their culture and clothing. The aim was to give female supporters visibility and a sense of belonging, as statistics showed that one in four fans of the Premier League were female (but largely absent from sports media of the day). Appropriating the look and feel of self-published football fanzines created by male fans in the 1980s, GIRLFANS was specifically designed to be rolled up and put in a pocket. The first issue, created in the 2013/14

season at Anfield, featured forty-eight pages of Liverpool supporters: ordinary fans, some from Liverpool and others from France, China and Malaysia. On one page a woman is wearing a red hijab and Liverpool scarf; another woman's face is obscured by the replica European Cup she is holding, and in another photograph by GIRLFANS' co-photographer Alex Hurst, an eighty-year-old woman is dressed head to toe in red. Her collection of pin badges is an emblem of her lifelong support of the club.[5]

Pages from the GIRLFANS zine

Football

Later zines celebrated the women and girls of Everton, Manchester City (in collaboration with City's research team), Burnley (an issue for the British Textile Biennial) and Celtic (a 'green and white' issue, with written contributions from fan-activist group On The Ball). In 2018, Bury supporter and photographer Zoë Hitchen produced a special issue of *GIRLFANS*, focusing on a football crowd without a home. The murky underbelly of football ownership meant that Bury FC had been expelled from the English Football League due to financial mismanagement, marking the demise of a club with a 133-year history.[6] To keep the story of the club and its fans in the news, a group of diehard 'Shakers' found their way into a ghostly Gigg Lane for what was to be their last time; the day was documented and published at Design Manchester's *We Are Bury* exhibition, curated by Hitchen. At the time of writing, Gigg Lane remains closed.

GIRLFANS' 'femorabilia' followed, in the form of pin badges to be worn at the match, a token of protest, solidarity and hope featuring feminised versions of popular football songs, chants and (infamous) flags taken straight from the terraces of Anfield, Gigg Lane and Old Trafford – 'Football, Kids, Husband, in that order', and so on.[7]

The internet, the unprecedented rise of social platforms and the introspection of the #MeToo movement created a new wave of under-represented fans who began to voice their own thoughts and opinions and shape football culture. Effectively, crowds can now gather inside a stadium or online, or do both at the same time, and women wearing replica shirts on Instagram or Facebook are now commonplace, their identity as 'authentic' football fans in stark contrast to a decade earlier. These new networks allow women to support each other and open routes for conversation and collaboration and to effect change across a myriad of channels: petitions, podcasts, publications, art, or simply a group chat on WhatsApp.

The publication and online platform *SEASON*, created by Felicia Pennant in 2015, champions female fans, football and fashion, and in response to the 'pale, male and sometimes stale' view of football, Pennant has found a niche for directional editorial and striking covers showcasing the key players in

Part of *Fan.Tastic Females ~ Football Her.Story*

women's football.[8] This Fan Girl, an online and offline community for female fans, launched in 2016, has collaborated with clubs and brands to change the perception of female fans. Their collaboration with the Carabao Cup in 2018 resulted in a campaign, 'We Are Female Fans', to show real faces of diverse fans in direct response to the misrepresentation of women as 'sexy fans' at the FIFA World Cup in Russia.[9] This Fan Girl also hosts informal meet-ups and watch-parties, where like-minded women can connect and discuss the game. Her Game Too has also gained the attention of clubs and fans, as a movement that hopes to eradicate sexism in football. By asking female fans to report abuse directly to them, Her Game Too acts as a conduit between fans and their clubs, thus circumnavigating governing bodies, who can appear to address such issues at a glacial pace. Significantly, at the beginning of 2022, more than sixty clubs have officially partnered with them from several tiers of the English and Scottish leagues.[10]

In Europe, *Fan.tastic Females ~ Football Her.story* is a touring exhibition of photographs and films depicting female fans and produced by volunteers from a broad range of clubs. The work promises to show the realities of fan.tastic women.[11] In Rotterdam, journalist Ellen Mannens questions why Feyenoord's small but fanatical female fan base engage in a world where men make up the majority, in her series *365 Feyenoordvrou* (365 Feyenoord Women).[12]

Football Without Fans Is Nothing

Photos from the Bomboneras Instagram feed

Football

Labelled by MUNDIAL as 'the best Instagram account on the planet', Bomboneras by Pancho Monti shows the pictorial journey of iconic Boca Juniors jerseys, worn by a series of the club's female fans. Their image of ninety-one-year-old Lilita soon went viral; her liveliness and witty facial expression captured the imagination of supporters the world over.[13] This unique glimpse into the world of Latin American football crowds, the likes of which most of us will never experience, is supposed to hold less importance and meaning for women, but the bonding and collective solidarity in these overtly masculine spaces is evident in Erica Voget's stunning project 'Cuerpas Reales Hinchas Reales' (Real Bodies, Real Fans).[14] The ongoing portrait project 'seeks to portray female fans and dissidents from different football clubs in order to make them visible in this historically masculinised environment'. Since its beginnings in 2019, Voget has created a network of more than eighty female photographers, who are invited to work with a particular fan base. Starting in Argentina, Uruguay and Chile, her call to action has been answered further afield, in Berlin and Spain.[15] What is perhaps particularly moving is how older women are being portrayed in all of the work mentioned: their hidden faces, voices and overall contribution to football is finally being acknowledged.[16]

Other initiatives, too, are catering to those who are not regular members of a crowd. Founded in 2017 by Jacqui Forster, Women at the Game (WATG) offered matchday experiences to women who had never been to football or had few friends interested in the game. Choosing to meet at coffee shops for a pre-match cappuccino instead of a pint helped to offer an environment more inclusive for women of different faiths, women with children or women who had never experienced a live game.[17] The scheme was supported by clubs at all levels, and a WATG gathering hosted by Manchester City was a first taste of live football for some of the women. With the knowledge that the group would be sitting together, the party moved to the Etihad and to the turnstiles, where a problem with the tickets meant that the group was temporarily not allowed inside the stadium. The short delay prompted some unwanted comments from men in the queue behind them: an example, if it was needed, that for the new football fans, WATG was indeed a supportive and sound idea.[18]

Fans have long used the power of crowds and their shared identity to campaign for causes important to them, with one example being the criticism of the corporatisation of English football, a recurring polemic that highlights fans as the true custodians of football clubs. Tensions between clubs, fans and football's governing superpowers are regularly stoked by the rampant commercialisation of football, with ticket prices a particular cause of disagreement. A charged atmosphere and the support of the mystical twelfth man has the power to suck a ball into the opposition's net, but equally the sight of the twelfth man (all 10,000 of them) leaving the ground, in protest at a proposed ticket increase, is just as forceful. During the dark days of the near-catastrophic Hicks and Gillett era at Liverpool Football Club, a group of supporters met to discuss the future of their club in the Sandon public house, the very spot where the club was formed.19 From this meeting a supporters' union, Sons of Shankly, evolved, creating a more unified voice in the battle for the club's future. Following a successful sale of the club, the new custodians, Fenway Sports Group, were also given a taste of this collective action. In a 2016 Premier League match against Sunderland FC, the coordinated walk-out in the seventy-seventh minute, which was prompted by plans to introduce a seventy-seven-pound match ticket, was the first of its kind in the club's history. The protest forced owners Fenway Sports Group to perform a swift U-turn on ticket prices. Deciding to change their name to the more inclusive 'Spirit of Shankly', more recently they have initiated a historic Supporter's Board model, with affiliates: LFC Women's Supporters Club, Liverpool Disabled Supporters Association, Spion Kop 1906 and Kop Outs, the LGBT+ fan group for LFC supporters, ensuring improved fan representation in future discussions with the club.

It's no surprise, then, that this example of strength in unity between Spirit of Shankly and Everton's Blue Union, a coalition of fan groups – Evertonians for Change, Keeping Everton In Our City, The People's Group and SOS1878 – led to an important joint community initiative,

'Fans Supporting Foodbanks', fronted by a Red, Ian Byrne MP, and a Blue, Dave Kelly. What started as an idea to bolster local foodbanks now accounts for a quarter of all donations to North Liverpool Foodbanks, and the simple concept has inspired other clubs, including Premier League adversaries Manchester City, whose supporters liaised with Fans Supporting Foodbanks to instigate their own matchday collections. Using the hashtag #HungerDoesntWearClubColours, this is about solidarity, not rivalry.[20]

The most urgent issue that football has with itself is racism, in the crowd and on the field. The global governing bodies in football have always been worryingly off the pace in matters of equality, diversity and inclusion. In 2016, FIFA declared the end of its three-year anti-racism task force, stating it had 'fulfilled its mission'. Alarmingly, this came just before the 2018 FIFA World Cup in Russia, where people from LGBT+ communities and minority ethnic groups have long been the target of abuse.

In 2020, during the COVID-19 pandemic, people mobilised in a unified fight for justice and an end to racism after the callous murder of a Black man, George Floyd, by a police officer, Derek Chauvin, in Minneapolis. The brutal nature of Floyd's death unleashed collective outrage across the world, as did 'taking the knee' – a symbol first seen in America's NFL in 2016 when 49ers quarterbacks Colin Kaepernick and Eric Reid knelt on one knee during the national anthem. As an act of peaceful protest against oppression and police brutality it became a mark of solidarity and respect and was adopted by many footballers in the UK.[21] The issue remains, however, that FIFA's anti-discrimination policy is at odds with its profit-making business, and with the 2022 FIFA World Cup taking place in Qatar, there is clearly an uneven playing field when it comes to the rights of every human.[22]

●

Globally, there are numerous organisations and communities working against racism, sexism, homophobia, transphobia and far-right nationalism. FARE has a network of over 150 members (groups and individuals) and through its 'Football People' action week

grant supports fan-led diversity and inclusion activities.[23] Similarly 'Fans For Diversity', a grassroots project by the Football Supporters Association and Kick It Out, English football's equality and diversity organisation, recognises that the colour of the shirt is the only difference between football supporters. From conferences and photographic exhibitions,[24] to the development of the LGBT+ fans' group network Pride In Football, they are shaping modern fan culture for the better.

An example of a small grassroots campaign with a substantial impact emerged when three Celtic supporters, Erin Slaven, Mikaela McKinley and Orlaith Duffy, buoyed by the repeal of the Offensive Behaviour at Football and Threatening Communications (Scotland) Act, a campaign they had actively taken part in, decided to petition Celtic to supply free sanitary products in the toilets at Celtic Park. Their argument was simple: men didn't pay for soap or toilet paper, so why should women have to pay for period products? In an approach which reflected the very ethos of the club's founding father, socialism and football were clearly intertwined and Celtic would be the ideal club to implement their idea. Collectively named On The Ball, they were supported by Labour MSP Monica Lennon, who had proposed a bill for free sanitary products in Scotland. The petition led to a meeting with Celtic, who announced an immediate trial at the ground. Despite some expected trolling on Twitter, the trio remained steadfast, and the campaign message spread outside of Scotland – first to Tranmere Rovers, then to more than a hundred clubs in England, Ireland and the US. Both equality and equity were important to the campaign, which supplied fans with email templates so they could engage with their own club: an example of fan-led activism at its finest. Though On The Ball came to a natural end in 2020, its impact continues to benefit female supporters and it has also helped to destigmatise conversations around menstruation. Scotland went on to become the first country in the world to make period products free for all, in 2020.[25]

While the pages that follow revel in the finer points of stadium design, under-representation in the crowd, on the football field, in the director's box, in football governance and in architecture itself has meant that insight into the fans' lived experiences and their relationship with the design process has historically been overlooked. Having enough toilets is always a priority for women, and the availability of free sanitary products shows that clubs are now listening to them. Good lighting when leaving a stadium after a night game and plenty of safe transport options are essential, and strategies to counter anti-discriminatory behaviour are still, unfortunately, a necessity. Protecting personal space is important to many supporters whether they are seated or standing, and as mentioned above, the mere thought of navigating turnstiles can be a literal barrier to being part of a crowd. As stadiums in the top leagues become more Disneyfied and financially unattainable for many, the research and examples given here suggest that the foundations of a well-designed space should always be viewed through an intersectional lens. Putting the lure of a heated seat to one side, it's often the small yet practical details that make a stadium a home.

1   Jean Williams, *The History of Women's Football* (Barnsley: Pen & Sword History, 2021), pp. 96, 120, 136.

2   The Football Supporters' Association, 'Women at the Match', 24 November 2021, thefsa.org.uk/wp-content/uploads/2021/11/Women-at-the-Match-report.pdf [accessed 10 January 2022].

3   The Anfield Wrap, 'Women in Football – Fan Experiences: TAW Special', 28 July 2021, www.theanfieldwrap.com/2021/07/podcast-women-football-fan-experiences [accessed 10 January 2022].

4   Stacey Pope, *The Feminization of Sports Fandom: A Sociological Study* (New York: Routledge, 2017), p. 32.

5   girlfans.co.uk [accessed 10 January 2022].

6   National Football Museum, 'Football Fan Culture in 11 Museum Objects', 17 June 2020, youtu.be/AW91wSaGtdw [accessed 10 January 2022].

7   Felicia Pennant, 'The Best Women's World Cup 2019 Merch', www.vogue.co.uk/gallery/best-womens-world-cup-2019-merch [accessed 10 January 2022].

8   *SEASON*, www.season-zine.com [accessed 10 January 2022].

9   Alan Seymour and Paul Blakey, *Digital Sport Marketing : Concepts, Cases and Conversations* (London: Routledge, 2021), p. 108.

10 Sophie Hurcom, 'Her Game Too: The campaign to tackle sexism within football', 2 September 2021, www.bbc.co.uk/sport/football/58360698 [accessed 10 January 2022].

11 Fan.tastic Females, www.fan-tastic-females.org [accessed 10 January 2022].

12 *365 Feyenoordvrou*, www.365feyenoordvrouwen.nl/365feyenoordvrouwen [accessed 10 January 2022].

13 Ludo Romagnoli, 'Bomboneras is the best Instagram account on the planet', 2020, mundialmag.com/blogs/articles/bomboneras-pancho-monti-boca-juniors-interview [accessed 10 January 2022].

14 Christopher Thomas Gaffney, *Temples of the Earthbound Gods: Stadiums in the Cultural Landscapes of Rio de Janeiro and Buenos Aires* (Austin: University of Texas Press, 2008), p. 30.

15 Erica Voget, 'Cuerpas Reales Hinchas Reales', www.ericavoget.com/cuerpasreales [accessed 10 January 2022].

16 Anna Kessel, 'Groundbreaking women's football conference highlights buried stories', 8 March 2018, www.theguardian.com/football/2018/mar/08/womens-football-conference-highlight-past-achievements [accessed 10 January 2022].

17 Suzanne Wrack, 'Women at the Game: Jacqui Forster's inspirational football mission', www.theguardian.com/football/2017/oct/31/women-at-the-game-jacqui-forster [accessed 10 January 2022].

18 The author attended the WATG event and Champions League match between Manchester City and FC Basel (7 March 2018).

19 Peter Millward, 'Reclaiming the Kop? Analysing Liverpool Supporters' 21st Century Mobilizations', *Sociology*, 46/4, 2012, pp. 633–648.

20 Melissa Reddy, 'Stronger Together: The social power of football in motion on Merseyside', www.joe.co.uk/sport/stronger-together-the-social-power-of-football-in-motion-on-merseyside-213366 [accessed 10 January 2022].

21 Amnesty International, 'Colin Kaepernick: Ambassador of Conscience', www.amnesty.org/en/latest/news/2018/04/colin-kaepernick-ambassador-of-conscience [accessed 10 January 2022].

22 Amnesty International, 'Qatar World Cup of Shame', www.amnesty.org/en/latest/campaigns/2016/03/qatar-world-cup-of-shame [accessed 10 January 2022].

23 FARE Network, '#FootballPeople weeks', www.farenet.org/campaigns/footballpeople-action-weeks [accessed 10 January 2022].

24 Fans For Diversity, 'My City, My Shirt', 5 January 2021, thefsa.org.uk/news/my-city-my-shirt [accessed 10 January 2022].

25 Katie Falkingham, 'Periods and football: Meet the fans campaigning for free sanitary products at stadiums', 21 August 2018, www.bbc.co.uk/sport/football/45262541 [accessed 10 January 2022].

Space and Emotion
Jacques Herzog

Football was a part of my life long before I was an architect. Growing up in Basel, our apartment was literally attached to the FC Basel stadium, the Landhof, which is still there, although it's no longer used as a football ground. I spent much of my youth there, and I even played football there. So as a Basel supporter, I was fully infected by the virus that is being a football fan. It's a special condition, being a supporter; it's a kind of sickness that you can't get rid of your entire life. I still have it today. And I think it's important to state this at the outset, because what makes football an amazing sport is the emotion – the moments of success and failure. And architecture, too – while on the one hand it is a highly rational business it is also, on the other, a highly emotional one. Great architecture has a lot to do with psychological moments. It touches our emotions and all our senses. This is especially true for stadiums: they are theatres for the emotions.

The first stadium that Herzog & de Meuron designed was for Basel – St Jakob-Park Stadium – twenty years ago. It was the first modern stadium in Switzerland, and it remains the largest. Naturally we invested a lot of passion and energy into that building, and it's where we tested a number of the spatial issues that would find their way into our later stadiums, such as the Allianz Arena in Munich. These come down to a few rules. Above all, we wanted to bring the fans and the pitch as close together as possible. I often compare it to a Shakespearean theatre, which triggers such an intense interaction between the actors and the audience. As an architect I was aware of how important it is in your home stadium to heighten the encounter between the performer and the viewer. Some of this we did by introducing colour – the red and blue of Basel. The red has the nobility of velvet, like you might find in an opera house or a theatre, and it has a particular intensity against the specific green of the pitch, so that it reinforces the perception of the pitch, where the action is. And the other crucial aspect is how you shape the roof to enclose the space. The roof helps concentrate the atmosphere. It turns the stadium into the cauldron where the meal is cooked.

When we designed the stadium in the late 1990s there were alternative projects on the table which I hated, not so much as an architect but as a supporter. I wanted badly to do the stadium just so that these other projects wouldn't be realised. There were plans to do a very light structure with a transparent roof. I would have hated that because all the heat evaporates, the whole energy escapes. But that was the spirit of stadiums at the time. It needed a supporter to design the stadium. There are not so many architects who are fans, who are passionate about that site and would see it as more than a mere design challenge. Pierre and I knew how to approach it because we knew, from our experience as supporters, that it needed to be an emotional space.

St Jakob remains one of my favourite stadiums, not least because, since it was built, Basel has won fourteen championships and really started to dominate Swiss football. But it's not just the team's success that makes me love the stadium; it's the way it has changed the demographic of the fans, allowing more families and children to attend. As a social space it is much more inclusive than it was when I was growing up. This is one of the most significant ways in which stadiums have changed in my lifetime. They were formerly sites of male pleasure, where you would drink beer and eat sausages, where there was standing room only and gravel on the ground. Whereas now they reflect a more open society that includes women and children, and, indeed, activities other than football. And I think this reflects how urban life in general has evolved over the last fifty years.

When thinking about designing a stadium, so much depends on the context – whether it nestles in a tight urban fabric, or whether it shines like a lantern on open ground. In a sense, you're not just designing a building but you're designing the approach to the building. Early on, stadiums were like chapels built into the neighbourhood. They might be attached to row houses or apartment blocks, totally integrated into daily life. Having said that football is an emotional and psychological experience, it is also bound to the ground, to a certain territory. And this was very much the case with our design for Chelsea's stadium at Stamford Bridge (which is currently on hold, but we hope will be realised one day). The design grows out of that particular territory of a Victorian brick terraced neighbourhood. We conceived the stadium as a cathedral-like building, with tall, almost Gothic brick buttresses. As a form it strives to be both archaic and contemporary at the same time.

If you transplanted Stamford Bridge to the suburbs of Munich, where the Allianz Arena is, it would look absurd. Whereas because the Allianz Arena sits in a very open, peri-urban condition, between the airport and the city, it wanted to be a light, airy object – a lantern in the landscape. You approach it completely differently, walking from the car park or from the train station. We choreographed the approach, creating a landscape of meandering paths that allow people to choose different routes to the stadium. The flow of people is like a religious procession; it has a ceremonial quality.

If you are building a stadium within a city centre, as at Stamford Bridge, then the approach is coloured by and funnelled through all of the surrounding life. And as a civic space, the stadium ideally wants to be inhabited by that street life, so that it's not just a place for football but a place for daily life. It's somehow ridiculous for a stadium to be a place where a match happens once or twice a week and is empty the rest of the time. You want to drill holes in the stadium's crust and fill them with life – cafés, kindergartens, whatever people need. Architecture is the art of bringing things together so that they work both economically and socially, so that football and the other needs of the community do not need to be mutually exclusive.

One of the stadiums that has impressed me the most is Anfield, where Liverpool play. When we won the commission to design Tate Modern in the late 1990s, one of the first things I did was to go and see a match at Anfield, because I wanted to experience this quintessentially English form of public space. And so even when I was designing a museum I was thinking about football. At Anfield it's not the architecture itself that is impressive – there is nothing particularly beautiful about it – it's the atmosphere. As an architect you might say I should be looking at the design but in fact I'm looking at the fans, because even in boring stadiums great fans make a wonderful spectacle. The fans have a very powerful choreographic and spatial impact. You could almost say that the fans are the space of the stadium. And if there are no fans then the stadium just looks sad. It can look like the Colosseum, which one can enjoy empty as a piece of archaeology, but it's the people who make the music. And that is also true of architecture in general, and especially of plazas and public spaces.

So when designing a stadium, thinking of the choreography comes first: how people move towards the stadium, and then how they move into it and through it. I think about the relationship between the spectator and the player. And about sensory qualities – how are the acoustics; can smell become a factor and where? How should the space be conceived? There is no rule for that as such, but everything we have done in our designs so far was to focus and intensify the experience. Because that is the ingredient that makes the game so attractive and different from virtual games. The fans may or may not be aware of how the stadium is constructed to be a kind of a theatre, that it is a composition of elements designed to enhance the pleasure of the game, but the evidence is all around them.

Jacques Herzog was interviewed by Justin McGuirk

St Jakob-Park, Basel, Switzerland, Herzog & de Meuron, 1996–2002

Space and Emotion

A View from the Pitch:

The Cathedrals of the People
Martino Simcik Arese

Martino Simcik Arese is the COPA90 STORIES editor and an expert on fan culture across the globe. Part activist, part journalist, part fan, Martino has travelled the world to tell stories about the things that happen when people gather in crowds to watch football. His films, articles and work provide an exclusive look behind the scenes of some of the most obscure, politically aware and socially vital football fan groups in some of the most under-reported locations that host football matches.

●

Olympique Marseille football fans celebrate a goal during a game at the Stade Velodrome, Marseille, France, 2006

If an alien were dropped on planet Earth, and they asked to see an example of the highest form of human experience, when it comes to why members of our species so deeply identify with their local space and the place they are from, I would tell that alien to visit a football stadium.

Whichever stadium you go to, or team or competition you watch, there'll be a different melody to the cacophony of noise. But the fan rituals – things such as the way they walk to the ground, the discussions afterwards, the subcultures – are often very much the same. Looking at, and being part of, a football crowd is perhaps a more intense example of local identity than anything else.

In these places where crowds exist, there is a heightened sense of belonging that you can't find elsewhere. Humans haven't built anything that gives the same sense of regular and communal togetherness outside of religion or being a part of something considered a higher order. These are places where you can hug and embrace a complete stranger, to celebrate something that is understood as a shining beacon in the monotony of life outside the stadium. There can be a sense of meaning here beyond life itself. And that's wonderful.

One of the most amazing moments you can experience as part of a football crowd is the feeling of confronting authority in whatever form it may take, where there is a sense of a community keeping each other safe against what is perceived to be a collective enemy. It can be so visceral, violent and dangerous, and you can of course delve into the morality of particular situations, but living it and being among it is an irreplaceable feeling.

Modern stadiums have been commercialised and expanded in line with the game, and often it's the ways that fans react to this trend that is most interesting. In different grounds, in different parts of the world, it's about the local graffiti; the different local snacks and food that people sell in front of the stadiums – arancini and salamella in Italy, or the sunflower seeds in the Balkans that are roasted and salted in different ways which are hyper-specific to each area; it's the stickers designed by fans that appear on the backs of seats and on bathroom mirrors. The curve, shape and design of the stadium structure will always affect how noise travels, but those little quirks in and around the stadiums that have been created by people themselves are what make a community feel that the stadium belongs to them.

In places that are designed for tens of thousands of people to be in at the same time, the most bizarre and strange things can happen. The most surprising thing I've ever seen was at Sassuolo's Mapei Stadium in Reggio Emilia, Italy. The stadium was designed at a time when hooliganism was of huge concern, and a water-filled moat was built to run between the players on the grass and the fans in the stands, essentially to prevent pitch invasions. The moat is pretty deep, and the water for it runs in from a local river. I once watched some bored fans catch a fish out of the moat mid-game. Insane.

Martino Simcik Arese was interviewed by James Bird

A View from the Pitch

A View from the Pitch:

It's a Carnival
Camila Rojas

Boca Juniors' stadium, La Bombonera, is a mythical, wondrous, bubbling place. The Buenos Aires club, formed in 1905 by Italian immigrants mostly from Genoa, is rooted in the working-class communities that surround it in a football-obsessed city that is thought to have the highest concentration of football clubs in the world. Boca's main rival, a club called River Plate, is only seven kilometres down the road. Boca is the club of blue and yellow, of the nurture of Diego Maradona, of a stadium nicknamed 'the Chocolate Box' because of its shape. But as much as anything else, Boca Juniors is known for its fans.

Intense. All-encompassing. Loving. On matchday, the surrounding roads become a river of blue and yellow passion, and when the fans in the LA 12 section of the ground jump together and sing, the stands will physically sway in a motion that has led to the phrase 'La Bombonera no tiembla, late' ('The Bombonera does not tremble, it beats').

Camila Rojas is a thirty-one-year-old Boca Juniors fan, and like so many Boca fans, the club is her life.

●

The first thing that comes to my mind when I think about Boca is my parents. Especially my dad. When I was really young, we used to watch videos together of Diego Maradona playing football, just to get to sleep.

I went with my dad to La Bombonera for the first time on my tenth birthday on 7 March 2001. We were in the first round of the Copa Libertadores, a South American competition between all the best clubs from across the continent, and we were playing against a Colombian team called Deportivo Cali. I remember so much about that day.

I felt so very little compared to everything else around me, and I was walking with a flag that was double my size! Although we went to the ground early because it was my first time, the streets were completely full with other people heading towards the match. I'll never forget walking towards our stand and seeing how big the stadium was for the first time. I cried, hugged my dad, and became so excited.

Looking back now, I understand that it's a feeling that has lasted forever, a feeling that comes from the amount of collective energy you get from a group of the same people coming together to support the same team. The stadium and the crowd that fills it represent Argentinian culture: the streets painted with bright colours, the stands alive with noise, the smells of people and food.

Often, when I go to the stadium, I spend hours watching the people and crowds in the stands more than the football game itself. I love to look at everyone's faces, to feel that we're all part of the same family. There is a feeling in the stands at La Bombonera that it doesn't matter where you think you belong: this is an open space for football passion. There are moments where you hug strangers and it feels like you've known them for ever, but it's likely you'll never see that person again. That magic is what brings this football team to the people; there is a passion here that goes beyond normal boundaries.

Going to watch Boca isn't just football. It's a carnival.

Camila Rojas was interviewed by James Bird, photograph by Pancho Monti

A View from the Pitch

Colchester United fan rattle, used during
Colchester v. Arsenal,
24 January 1959, FA Cup fourth
round, Roly Smith, 1959

Football rattles are ratchet devices
used to make a loud noise. Comprising
a gearwheel and stiff board mounted
to a handle, the board clicks against
the teeth of the gearwheel when the
handle is swung around. Ratchets were a
common fixture on UK football terraces
up until the 1970s, when increased
violence among fans led to the rattles
being banned for fear of them being
used as weapons.

Football

Dortmund, Andreas Gursky, 2009
C-Print, Diasec. Andreas Gursky, VG BILD-KUNST, Bonn.

Crowds

Football

TOP

Ukrainian fans, Serbia v. Ukraine
friendly, 2016

BOTTOM

Boca Juniors fans, Libertadores Cup
semi-finals, 2005

Organised fan groups are a powerful
presence in most football stadiums.
Taking different forms across the globe,
the most widely adopted model is that
of the Ultras, who are known for their
extreme dedication to their club and
impressive choreographies. Ultras
usually have a core team of founders who
coordinate the group's activities. Ultras
are often confused with hooligans, a type
of football fandom originating in the UK
where members actively seek out violent
confrontation with opposing supporters.
While various Ultras groups have engaged
in violent behaviour, their primary purpose
is to provide conspicuous shows of support
to their team. This can extend to include
particular social or political ideologies
and, in recent years, has come to include
large-scale protests against football's
increasing commercialisation. The origins
of the Ultras movement are contested.
Torcida Split in Croatia is widely
acknowledged as the longest-running
supporters' group of this type.

Crowds

St Pauli fans, Munich v. St Pauli, 2016

A *tifo* is a choreographed display produced by Ultras, usually created by collectively raising a large banner or by simultaneously holding up signs that together form a large image. The term comes from the Italian verb *tifare*, which means 'to support' or 'to be a fan of'. Footballing folklore often links it to the Italian for typhus, a bacterial infection that causes a fever, as participants in *tifos* are said to be gripped by a similarly intense fever. *Tifos* are generally reserved for important matches, such as cup finals, derbies or club anniversaries. They can take months or even years to organise and demand incredible commitment from participants, as routines are often practised for several hours a week in the lead-up to a one-off performance.

Football

Coligay fans at the Olympic stadium
in Porto Alegre, c.1977–83

Organised football fandom has
traditionally been an almost exclusively
male, heterosexual arena. This has been
challenged in recent years as more
diverse groups of fans have fought to
create and legitimise their own spaces
within the stadium. This movement
has been greatly helped by the rise in
popularity of professional women's
football, as the women's game carries a
long history of accessibility and inclusion,
particularly for LGBTQ+ supporters.
    Historical examples of diverse
organised fan groups also exist within the
men's game. Coligay was a Brazilian fan
group formed in 1977, predominantly by
men who identified as homosexual. They
supported Grêmio, a club in Porto Alegre,
and for five years were a respected part
of the club's fanbase, producing loud,
colourful and original displays.

Crowds

Aerial view of Wembley Stadium, London, during the 1923 FA Cup Final between Bolton Wanderers and West Ham United which Bolton won 2–0. It was the first final held at Wembley and an estimated 200,000 people attended, overflowing onto the pitch.

Football has a long history of stadium disasters. There have been eight tragic instances, since the Ibrox tragedy of 1902, in which fifty or more people have lost their lives. The highest death toll to date occurred during a match in 1964 between Argentina and Peru at Lima's Estadio Nacional, where 328 people were killed and 500 injured as a result of crowd crushes.

Stadium disasters have been caused by a combination of factors, including staffing issues, unexpected or dramatic events on the pitch, and even adverse weather conditions. The common denominator, however, is the architecture of the stadium itself. A well-designed stadium should take account of the risk factors that might contribute towards unexpected crowd surges, preventing crushes or other disruptions.

Scottish architect and engineer Archibald Leitch was often hailed as the grandfather of football stadium design. Between 1899 and 1939, he partly or wholly designed stadiums across the UK and Ireland, including those for Arsenal, Aston Villa, Chelsea, Liverpool, Manchester United, Preston North End, Glasgow Rangers, Sunderland, Tottenham Hotspur and Wolverhampton Wanderers.

Leitch's first football commission was the new ground for his boyhood team, Rangers. His design for Ibrox Park was completed in 1899. The overall capacity of the new stadium was 75,000, making it the largest in the world at the time, but tragedy following its opening meant the capacity was quickly reduced. The first time that the new stadium was tested by a capacity crowd was on 5 April 1902, when Ibrox Park hosted a Scotland v. England game. Shortly after kick-off, a top section of the wooden terracing gave way, causing 125 people to fall more than fifteen metres to the ground below. Twenty-five people were killed and a further 517 were injured in the ensuing rush to escape. Although no individual was held legally responsible, it was agreed that the wooden terracing needed to at least double the number of joists in order to be able to hold the stated capacity.

Photographs taken in the wake of the Ibrox
disaster, 5 April 1902

Crowds

Patent no. GB190604453A, 'An Improved Method of Constructing the Terracing and Accessories thereof in Football and other Sports Grounds', Archibald Leitch, 1905

After the Ibrox disaster, Leitch persuaded Rangers to let him build the replacement stand. He created slopes of earth to support the tiered structure, a method used for many other stadium designs. Subsequent designs included a greater number of aisles to make it easier to enter and exit the stands, and these were sunken to dissuade fans from standing in them to watch the game. The disaster inspired Leitch to design and patent a tubular-steel crush barrier, which he believed would help prevent future stampedes.

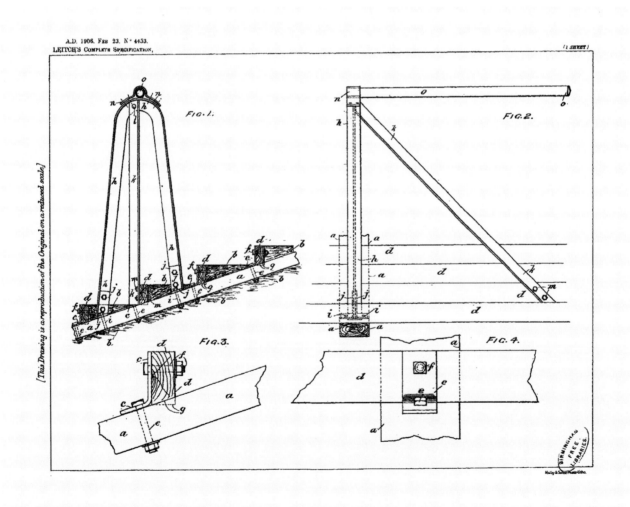

Fans walking away from Ibrox Park after
Rangers v. Celtic, 1963

Crowds

Despite the Ibrox disaster, Leitch went on to design twenty stadiums across the UK and Ireland. His experience as a factory architect allowed him to build large structures quickly and cheaply. He developed his own distinctive style, using a limited range of industrial materials.

A typical feature of his design was the two-tiered stand with criss-crossed steel balustrades on the upper tier, covered by a series of pitched roofs and occasionally a central gable. Another recurrent feature was a cottage-style pavilion to house dressing rooms, a boardroom, a manager's room and a gym. Craven Cottage, the pavilion after which Fulham's ground is named, is the only surviving example of this style.

The East Stand at Tottenham Hotspur's ground, White Hart Lane, London, during construction, July 1934

Football

Crowds

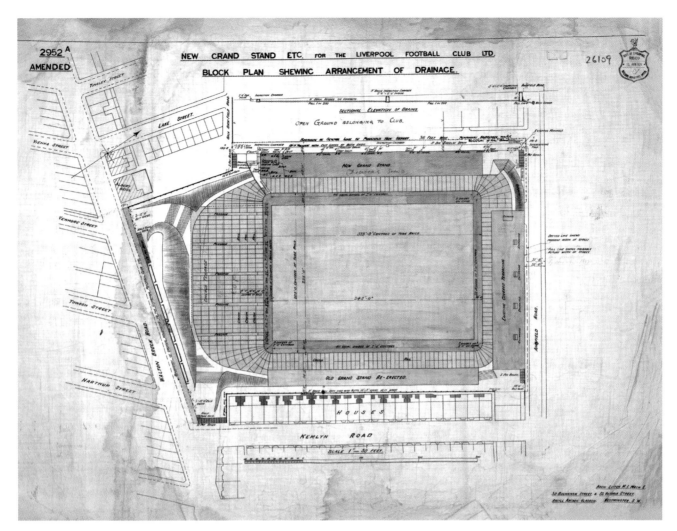

New grandstand for Liverpool FC,
Archibald Leitch, 1906

Football

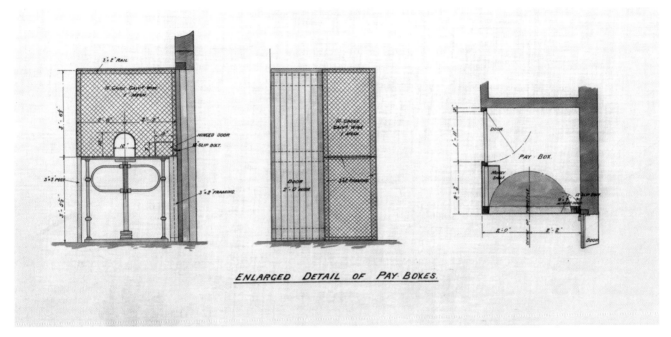

ENLARGED DETAIL OF PAY BOXES.

Details of doors, windows and pay boxes,
Anfield Stadium, Liverpool, Archibald
Leitch, 1906

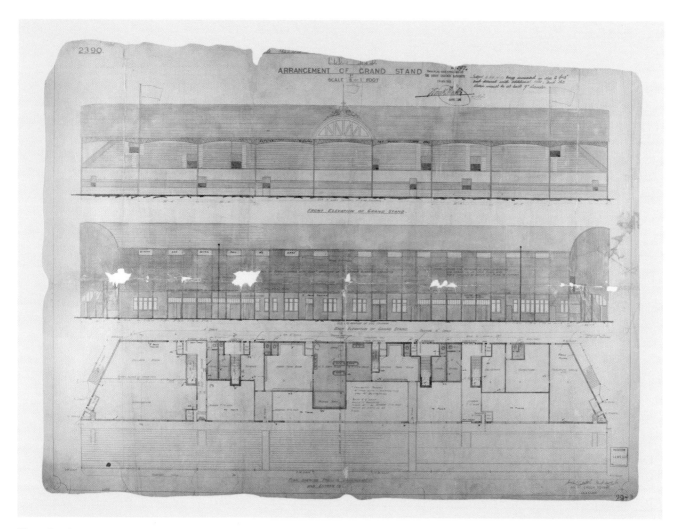

Plans for the grandstand at Ayresome
Park, Middlesbrough,
Archibald Leitch, 1903

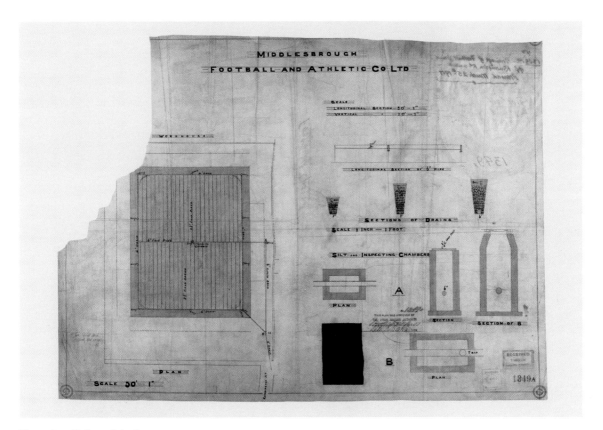

Plans for pitch and drainage,
Middlesbrough Football Club,
Archibald Leitch, 1907

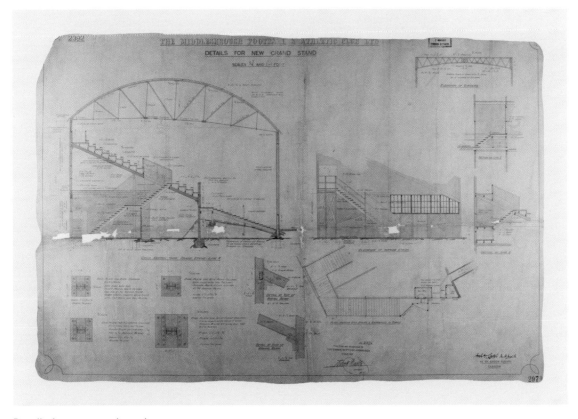

Details for new grandstand,
Middlesbrough Football Club,
Archibald Leitch, 1903

Crowds

The 1980s saw a spike in stadium disasters, with six separate events across the globe claiming the lives of about 335 people. While each event was caused by its own unique set of circumstances, the common factor was a lack of investment in stadium infrastructure. This was particularly true in the UK, where stadium design had remained relatively unchanged since the lifetime of Archibald Leitch. Along with the rise in hooliganism, this saw football wrongly vilified as an unattractive, crude and violent remnant of British working-class culture. In 1985, *The Sunday Times* newspaper described the game as 'a slum sport played in slum stadiums, and increasingly watched by slum people'.

RIGHT

Arsenal v. Chelsea, c.1985

Football

Crowds

TOP

Chelsea supporters at
Chelsea v. Millwall game,
4 February 1985

BOTTOM

Manchester United supporters,
1 March 1977

Crowds

Since the Hillsborough disaster in 1989, all-seated football stadiums have become standard in many other parts of the world. The cost of updating and maintaining grounds has led to increased ticket prices. Architects of new football stadiums must tread a fine line between reflecting the emotional significance of each ground and the financial reality of running a safe and efficient site.

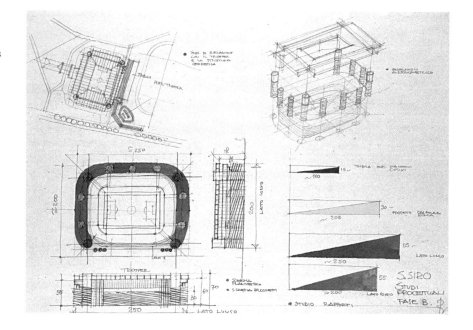

THIS SPREAD AND OVERLEAF

Stadio San Siro, Milan, Italy, Ragazzi and Partners, 1990

Stadio Giuseppe Meazza, commonly known as San Siro, is the home of both AC Milan and Internazionale. It is the largest stadium in Italy and one of the largest in Europe, with a seating capacity of 80,018. It was constructed in three stages, each increasing the capacity through the layering of stands and circulation spaces. The third stage of San Siro's development coincided with Italy hosting the 1990 FIFA World Cup. Although it was initially intended that the old stadium would be demolished and rebuilt, the existing structure was updated due to time and financial constraints. Architect Giancarlo Ragazzi, architect Enrico Hoffer and engineer Leo Finzi designed a third ring of seats along three sides of the stadium, supported by eleven concrete towers. Each tower was wrapped in a spiral walkway, echoing the long ramps of the existing outer shell and creating a hypnotic sense of procession around the building. This showcased a new, creative approach to stadium design.

Football

Crowds

Crowds

Tottenham Hotspur Stadium, London
Populous, 2019

Opened in 2019, Tottenham Hotspur
Stadium was built on the site of
White Hart Lane, Tottenham's home
ground from 1899 to 2017. The move
to all-seated stands had dramatically
reduced the capacity of the original
stadium, so it was demolished. The new
ground is now the largest club stadium
in London, with a capacity of 62,850.
It features a tight oval-shaped bowl
with steeply angled stands, allowing
spectators to be closer to the pitch and
creating a more intense atmosphere.
Tottenham Hotspur's new stadium
includes a fully retractable pitch that
can be used for both football and NFL
(National Football League) American
football games. The stadium is the
first venue in Europe purpose-built
for the NFL and enables the club to
generate additional revenue. The pitch
is maintained by a head groundsperson
and fifteen full-time assistants.

Football

Allianz Arena, München-Fröttmaning,
Germany, Herzog & de Meuron, 2001–5

Allianz Arena is a football stadium
outside Munich, Germany, with a
capacity of approximately 70,000.
It was initially designed to be the home
of two local teams, Bayern Munich
and 1860 Munich, but since 2017 it
has been solely occupied by Bayern
Munich. The stadium has three defining
characteristics: an inflatable outer
shell that can be illuminated at night;
long, processional walkways built into
the surrounding landscape; and a
crater-like interior. The illuminated
outer skin of the stadium is composed
of large, diamond-shaped ethylene
tetrafluoroethylene (ETFE) cushions.
ETFE is a fluorine-based plastic that
resists deterioration and keeps its
strength in a range of temperatures.
The colour of each individual cushion
can be controlled digitally, changing
the appearance of the stadium.
This initially allowed the building to
communicate which of its two resident
teams was playing, but it continues to
act as an architectural beacon across
the open landscape.

Football

Crowds

Stamford Bridge, London, UK
Herzog & de Meuron, concept, 2013

In 2017, planning permission was granted for the construction of a new 60,000-seater stadium to replace Stamford Bridge, the home of Chelsea. The new stadium concept is inspired by Westminster Abbey, with 264 brick piers set to enclose the existing structure and create a covered walkway around its perimeter. The brickwork, referencing local architecture, supports a steel ring above the pitch to cover the increased number of seats.

Football

Forest Green Rovers Eco Park stadium,
Stroud, Gloucestershire, Zaha Hadid
Architects, competition win 2016

In 2019, Zaha Hadid Architects were
granted planning permission to build the
world's first all-timber stadium. Home
to Forest Green Rovers, the stadium
embodies the club's environmentally
conscious ethos by using low-carbon
construction methods and operational
processes. Almost every element is
made of sustainably sourced timber
and the entire complex is powered by
sustainable energy. The design retains
and enhances the existing meadow
landscape of the site, creating a striking
landmark that is respectful of its
pastoral setting. Forest Green Rovers
were named the world's 'greenest'
football club after they reached carbon-
neutral status in 2017. Players have
adopted a vegan diet, while kits are
made of sustainably sourced materials
such as bamboo, recycled plastic and
recycled coffee grounds. The organic
grass pitch is watered with recycled
rainwater, while solar panels are used to
power floodlights. The club is chaired by
Dale Vince, founder of green electricity
company Ecotricity, and the new
stadium will form the centrepiece of a
new green technology business park.

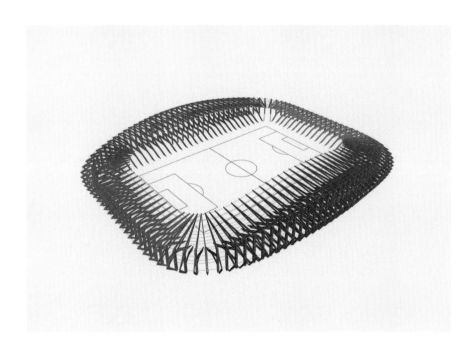

Crowds

Estádio Municipal de Braga, Portugal
Eduardo Souto de Moura
2000–3

Braga Municipal Stadium is the
30,286-capacity stadium in Braga,
Portugal, that is home to Sporting Clube
de Braga. Also known as 'A Pedreira'
(The Quarry), the stadium is carved into
the face of the adjacent Monte de Castro
and offers spectacular views of the
city below. Two concrete stands stretch
along the length of the pitch, their
cantilevered roofs connected by a series
of steel cables. The design was inspired
by ancient South American bridges built
by Incas. The building is positioned so
that those who can't afford a ticket can
watch from the surrounding hillside,
extending the sightlines beyond the
stadium itself.

Football

Crowds

Stadio Luigi Ferraris, Genoa, Italy,
designed by Vittorio Gregotti, 1987–9,
photographs by Matteo de Mayda, 2020

The Luigi Ferraris Stadium is a
36,600-capacity stadium in Genoa, Italy,
that is home to rival teams Genoa CFC
and UC Sampdoria. Originally opened
in 1911, the stadium was dismantled and
rebuilt before the 1990 FIFA World Cup
according to a new design by Vittorio
Gregotti. Drawing inspiration from the
surrounding neighbourhood, Gregotti
created a stadium that echoed the form
and colour of nearby housing. This series
of photographs was taken the day after
the architect's death from COVID-19,
at the age of 92.

Football

Crowds

Football

4

Spectacle

And It's Live …
Martin Tyler
interviewed by James Bird

JB: Just three weeks after King George V granted the BBC the Royal Charter on New Year's Day 1927, football as a spectacle changed forever. The match itself, a 1–1 draw between Arsenal and Sheffield United at Highbury, wasn't especially memorable, but the way that people situated outside of the ground found out about those two goals very much was. Tucked up in a wooden shed on the east side of the ground, former rugby player Henry Blythe Thornhill Wakelam and his assistant commentated on the game to households across the country. This was the first time a football match had been broadcast live on the radio.

To help those listening at home, producer Lance Sieveking created a diagram that split the pitch into eight numbered squares, with Wakelam's assistant calling out the number that corresponded to where the action was happening on the pitch. Listening back to the crackly recording now, it does sound slightly chaotic, but the accompanying diagram which was published in the *Radio Times* has gone down in folklore as the origin of the phrase 'back to square one'. Football fans do like to romanticise, though, and it's more likely that the phrase actually comes from the game of snakes and ladders or even hopscotch.

Martin Tyler in the commentary box, St Mary's Stadium, Southampton, 2002

It wasn't until over a decade after that first radio broadcast that football fans would be able to see the game from the comfort of their own homes, as well as hear it. The BBC first tested the technology involved in broadcasting football on the television in September 1937, with a match between Arsenal and Arsenal Reserves organised specifically for the event. The 1938 FA Cup final between Preston North End and Huddersfield Town became the first full match to be broadcast live on TV around a year later. There were over 93,000 in attendance at Wembley that afternoon, compared to the mere 10,000 people in the country with televisions in their houses.

Commentary box at Celtic Park, Glasgow, 2018

Football as a spectacle, of course, has changed greatly since that first broadcast. The numbers are staggering: over 320 million people watched England lose to Italy in the Euros final at Wembley in July 2020, for instance. The phenomenon of 'second screening' is now consistent across the world – with fans watching the game on one screen and doing something else connected to the game with another. In fact, according to a GlobalWebIndex study, fifty-one per cent of all fans watching FIFA World Cup matches in 2018 on TV were using social media at the same time. The real figure is probably higher.

Fans now watch games through Twitch streams and TikTok highlights. Bedroom tacticians analyse live as fans WhatsApp their friends the stats. Twitter users from across the world dictate opinion on individual players through hashtags. The new generation of football-obsessed teens – or FOTs – are beginning to move away from the tribal nature of supporting a club to the more individual nature of supporting a player. When Lionel Messi signed for Paris Saint-Germain in the summer of 2021, PSG's Instagram following went up from around 41 million to 44 million. The spectacle of the game is constantly in flux.

But one thing that has stayed the same over the ninety-five years of broadcast, as video assistant referees (VARs) and spider-cams and e-sports come to the fore, is the need for the commentator.

Everyone needs to know what's happening on the pitch. And Martin Tyler has seen it all.

Born in 1945, Martin has been calling games since the early 1970s and was voted the Premier League's Commentator of the Decade in 2003. He's covered the Champions League and the Premier League for Sky Sports since 1990, worked at every FIFA World Cup since 1978, and even lent his voice to the FIFA video game series for fifteen years. His voice is synonymous with watching football on the television in the UK, whether that's surrounded by your family in the sitting room, or sat in the pub on a Sunday with a roast.

A non-league footballer until his mid-twenties, Martin Tyler has been obsessed with the spectacle of the game since he was a child, and today combines his commentating with a coaching role at Woking FC – his boyhood club.

●

MT: I can remember being given my first football on Christmas Day when I was six or seven, and having it confiscated before the end of the day because I was kicking it around the house. I was in floods of tears, but I just wouldn't stop.

I went to Woking for the first time in December 1953 with the family from next door. We lived in little bungalows, and there were six kids next door, and one of them, he must have been eleven or twelve, asked me if I wanted to come to watch the football. I was given my bus fare and entrance money, and we just hopped on the bus from the end of the road and went straight to the club. I was pretty small back then, so I remember leaning over the barrier, one that's probably still there now, and watching Woking win 4–1. The next game I went to, just after Christmas, Woking lost 4–1, so I understood the highs and lows of being a football spectator very quickly. And I was hooked.

When Woking weren't playing, I started to get the train on my own to go and watch Chelsea or Fulham. I learned a lot about the culture of football fans and football during these times, being on trains with older people and learning about the humour and ways to talk about the game. I was a very impressionable young man going into a grown-ups' world ahead of schedule.

Looking back now, all of these things make the rest of my life rather fated.

My first interactions with football broadcasting were as a six-year-old. It was the FA Cup final, always a huge occasion, in May 1952 between Newcastle and Arsenal, and I remember being excited to find out that I could listen to the full game live via the airwaves in the family home. There were over 100,000 at the ground that day, and it was a year later that I recall watching a game on the television for the first time: a game that would go on to be known as 'The Match of the Century'.

On Wednesday 25 November 1953, England played an international friendly against a Hungary team that was ranked number one in the world, a team that featured one of the greatest players of all time in Ferenc Puskás. I remember watching that game on grainy footage as Kenneth Wolstenholme commentated in his understated and very accurate manner.

Hungary won 6–3, and the result is widely considered as the catalyst for the England national team changing everything about the way they trained and played, so quite a big 'first game' to see on the telly. The following year, I remember faking an illness at school – one of those stomach aches that can come on when you need to watch the football – for a televised match on the BBC between England and West Germany.

Already, I was aware of broadcasting and made sure I could get to football, whether it was in the flesh, watching on the television or listening to it on the radio.

There was a school playing field over the back of the fence at the bottom of our garden when I was growing up. We weren't supposed to go over to it, but we always did, and we'd use the hockey goalposts for goals. It's *goals* that have always fascinated me, since I was a kid.

I'd go and watch the local Saturday afternoon teams, too. After they'd arrived and put the nets up, they'd head back inside to get changed. That's when me and my friends would get ready to play. They'd be inside for twenty minutes or so, and even though we weren't supposed to, we'd run on to the pitch with a ball and just start whacking it into the back of the net until the adults came back out again and chased us away.

I suppose that's where the pocket diary on the playground came from. As a schoolkid, I'd use the section at the back of a diary I had where you were supposed to put addresses to write down every single goal I scored. I remember being on 499 goals by the end of the first term before breaking up for Christmas, and having to persuade enough of the other kids to play another game in order to make it a valid match in my eyes so that I could get to 500.

I've realised that by the time I got to university I knew much more about football than the subjects I was studying.

●

JB: After graduating from the University of East Anglia with a BA in Social Studies and an MA in Sociology, Martin continued to play football at a high level for Corinthian-Casuals in the Isthmian League. He was so obsessed with the game that he remembers going to parties with the players afterwards and asking the hosts if they had a television so that he could go downstairs to watch *Match of the Day*.

By May 1971, a twenty-five-year-old Martin got his first job in football after a tip-off from a girlfriend, who was beginning to think that he might be a 'deadbeat of a bet'. The publishers Marshall Cavendish gave him a staff writer role at the business. Each week he'd write a column on skills, tactics and training drills with with examples drawn by artists. Part of that routine were occasional visits to London Weekend Television studios to watch their tapes of players performing a particular skill.

After a childhood spent going to football matches on his own, noting down goals in the playground, and taking televisions downstairs at parties to watch *Match of the Day*, Martin was about to become part of broadcasting himself. In 1973, he got a role as a production assistant at London Weekend Television doing various things including interviewing football-ers on screen, and by 1974 a friend had asked him if he'd like to help commentate on a West Ham game. After using his weekends off to head to the gantry with legendary commen-tator Brian Moore and practise his own commentary, he finally got his turn.

●

MT: A call from Southern Television to one of my colleagues was made, and it went along the lines of 'We've got a game on 28 December. We don't have a commentator. Do you know anybody?' And so, they put my name forward.

Southampton v. Sheffield Wednesday on 28 December 1974, 3pm kick-off.

I was very, very nervous, but I got very lucky in several respects. Firstly, I hadn't seen Sheffield Wednesday play that season, so I got myself a room at the hotel where I knew they were going to be staying. It's an old commentator's trick, and I was a very young commentator, but I knew that maybe I would see them at breakfast or something like that. The manager Steve Burtenshaw saw me and said I could go and watch them train in the morning. So I went and got to know the team

a little better. Secondly, during the game itself, the first goal was early – usually not a good thing for a commentator – but it was scored by the only player with ginger hair, a guy called Eric Potts. This meant I'd be able to identify him straightaway. After the game the director, who was very well spoken, said to me, 'Well done, old boy. We've got another game in three or four weeks' time. Would you like to do that?' And, off the back of that, I always tell people that people have been telling me 'We've got another game …' ever since.

Having worked at London Weekend Television as an assistant producer ahead of this, I'd learned lots of little things that gave me a head start. One of the jobs I had was cutting ninety-minute recordings into high-light packages, and from this I'd taught myself the discipline of knowing when to speak, and when not to speak. If a commentator is too talkative, their voice will roll on between actions and make it difficult to edit. Obviously, technology now means that isn't a problem, but it taught me a lot in terms of utilising my voice only when needed.

I had to learn a technique called 'back-tracking' because the slow-motion replays back then were added on to the edit after-wards. This meant doing your recording 'blind', which means while the players were celebrating their goal, I'd be re-commentating on the goal that had just occurred. It wasn't until years later that I'd be able to see the replays happen in front of me on a screen.

Of course, cameras have changed massively too. Back then, we'd have maybe two main cameras, plus a low camera for close-ups, and cameras behind one of the goals. Now, we have over twenty, with their capabilities meaning the game looks like it does. But the microphones? They're still the same.

The Lip Microphone was invented in 1937 by the BBC and Marconi, and it includes a lip guard that means the speaker's mouth, and therefore voice, remains consistently at the same 2.25 inches away from the mic, meaning there's a stability to the sound. The labyrinth design also means that you can have winds up to around twenty miles per hour without them affecting speech, and any extraneous noise is stopped from coming in. The mic has been my tool and trade from day one to now;

it's a wonderful piece of kit. Sometimes, I'll be asked to go and do some pretend commentary for an advert or something, and if I arrive and they haven't got a Lip Mic, I'll tell them we'll have to find one otherwise it won't sound like me.

The other thing that hasn't changed is my 'hanging around' before a game – to soak the spectacle of it all in. Saying hi to the players, knowing when and who to speak to, saying hello when you arrive and then goodbye when you leave. I tell people it's like you're going into someone's house.

In terms of preparation, I often talk about the FIFA World Cup in Argentina in 1978, which was my first as a junior commentator. In the build-up, lots of the teams headed to Europe to play practice games, and we were given £500 to go around Europe and watch the relevant pre-tournament games. Mexico had a game against a club side in Germany called VfL Bochum, so I went along, and the Mexican captain scored a penalty. After the game, I did some of my hanging around the exit, and when he came out I said, in sort of pidgin Spanish, 'Always that side?', and he said, 'Always that side, to the goalkeeper's left!'

Weeks later, I'm commentating on my first ever game at a FIFA World Cup, and it's Mexico, and they get a penalty, and of course, the captain steps up to take it. So, before he took it, I took a deep breath and said into the microphone, 'He always puts it to the left hand side.' And he did. I'd somehow nailed my first ever World Cup goal.

●

JB: Having commentated for so many years on so many games on so many channels, Martin's voice is associated with the game's greatest moments. He was at Mexico in 1986 for Maradona's 'Hand of God' and Goal of the Century, immortalised Manchester City's Sergio Agüero's scintillating last-minute goal to secure the club its first Premier League win in 2012 with his 'AGUUUUEROOOOO!' call, and his commentary as Liverpool went 4-3 up on Newcastle in stoppage time in 1996 still gives me goosebumps.

His pre-kick-off 'And it's live!' is a familiar soundbite – a nod to his personal excitement and his knowledge of the spectacle he's creating for others, and a tribute to the years as a junior when he would be calling highlights and recorded games that weren't live.

●

MT: People often ask me about my favourite commentary moments, and they'll often shout them to me in the street, but it's not something I spend a lot of time thinking about. You can be overly sentimental and nostalgic, and I think that each moment of commentary is relevant to creating a very specific moment, and so I don't like to judge them historically, even if I don't mind other people doing it. People tell me that certain moments of commentary I've done have been iconic, but I honestly don't see it like that; as soon as a game is done, I'm thinking what's the next one? Where do I go next?

I still get a sort of out-of-body experience sat there, waiting for my name to be introduced before the game is handed over to me, and then knowing that I have to talk for at least fifty minutes without a break. That sense of excitement comes from the element of danger involved in commentating on a game of football. You might have all of your notes and preparation, and in theory there's a finite number of things that can happen, but there are so many variables to the game – and so many variables in your own brain, too.

Over the last forty-seven years, I hope we've brought something extra to the game for people who already enjoy it, and hopefully some who didn't were drawn in because of the way we broadcasters cover the game. Football has gone from back-page news to being worldwide front-page news, creating a common language that allows us all to speak to each other. I recall doing something with the Premier League years ago, where we looked at fans around the world who had to go to great lengths to watch their team's games on television. There were people who were doing things like running through desert terrain to get to a TV set to watch a match, and waking up at all sorts of times.

There is an extraordinary dedication and devotion to football that inspires us every time.

Martin Tyler was interviewed by James Bird

And It's Live …

A View from the Pitch:

A New Optimism
Reuben Dangoor

During England's successful 2018 World Cup run, Hackney-born artist and designer Reuben Dangoor captured the mood of a nation, and its team, exquisitely. For the first time in a long time, the England team seemed to reflect the mood of the younger generation. It was diverse, respectful, exciting, and Reuben's work was the antidote to what has often been an overbearingly negative national media. His reactive illustrations during the tournament were adored across the board, and here he tells us about how they were put together.

●

The concept of Britishness in football is very complicated, and can be difficult to articulate. Growing up, I watched lots of other countries around the world celebrate their national team in a way that seemed wholesome, but up until the World Cup in 2018, it hadn't felt right to do that with Britishness for some reason. It felt like positive nationalism was being shown by other countries, and it felt like there was always something here that held that back.

But that had changed by the time of the FIFA World Cup in 2018. It didn't feel so conflicted. It felt positive. It was a young, diverse team, and that's what made me able to celebrate it and make a virtue of it. I didn't want to shy away from the national flag, something with obvious conflicting meanings. In a sporting context, you should be able to leave all that behind and celebrate your team. I wanted to articulate a national pride that was free from the baggage, and it felt like the players were free from it that year. The expectation was high, but it wasn't pressure in the same way as before.

The Raheem Sterling illustration features Raheem standing with his hands behind his back and a St George's Cross blindfold across his eyes, with a series of cameras homing in on him. The media had been quite literally gunning for him after he got a tattoo of a gun on his leg earlier that year, to commemorate his father who was shot dead in Jamaica. Alongside the media going after him, there was also an expectation that he be able to perform on the pitch. I felt like I could

Raheem Sterling by Reuben Dangoor

communicate these double standards in my work.

With the illustration of the young Gareth Southgate as a player comforting the older Gareth Southgate as a manager, I felt like I could create something cathartic. Gareth missed a crucial penalty for England at Euro 96, and it's something that has lived long in football fans' memories. I can just about remember that penalty shoot-out happening, and then twenty-two years later I'm in a pub with England beating Colombia on penalties with him in charge. It felt significant: I wanted to show the redemption circle.

Generally, my work is quite detailed and finessed, but the World Cup pieces were done in a couple of hours. I'd begin with line drawings and then start getting colours on top so that I could get the message out there right away.

It's cool that people were so invested in the illustrations. They became a bit of an unofficial timeline of the tournament, and I had people asking what was coming next or what moment would be picked out from the previous match. I think it was the first time in my memory that England international football felt optimistic, and I wanted to be able to record and celebrate that with my work.

Reuben Dangoor was interviewed by James Bird

A View from the Pitch

A View from the Pitch:

Every Day Is A School Day
Statman Dave

Football fans have begun to demand more from broadcasting. The spectacle of the game has evolved from watching ninety minutes of two teams trying to beat each other, to fans wanting to consume complex mathematical data on possession stats via second screens, algorithms that calculate how many goals a team are expected to have scored, and live tactical analysis that reveals specific movements players are making at the request of their manager.

At the forefront of this movement is Statman Dave, a football data analyst who streams live and interactive videos on Twitch three times a week, and has over half a million people who follow his YouTube and social channels every single day. Dave's content will be watched for something like 55,000 hours and hit around 40 million impressions per month. The content is designed to have accessibility at its core, and his work has evolved from being created in his bedroom to being broadcast on the BBC and Sky, creating a global community of fans who learn more about the game with him every single day.

Statman Dave's logo links his output across all of his social media channels

My mum's love of watching football had a huge impact on me, and us getting a season ticket together at Old Trafford when I was small is something I'll always cherish. Around the same time, I started to get into something that probably changed the course of my life: the computer game *Football Manager*, or, as it was known then, *Championship Manager*. Statman Dave at ten years old was obsessed with that game. The detailed data side of it, the way the formations and tactics were designed on screen, and the way that the attributes of each player were graded from one to twenty completely captivated me.

After graduating in 2013, I started working in football data and began to realise that there was a gap in the analytical side of the game. Football fans are very opinionated, but I realised that there were fans who would also like to consume the spectacle of the game in the same way I did: through tactics.

My content might range from detailed pre-match tactics videos, to tweets during games that give stats about the players or teams, and broadcasts analysing managers' philosophies and what we can learn from watching their teams.

We have a partnership with a company called InStat, a video-driven platform that allows us to watch specific moments that help form our analysis. We can search for every single touch Lionel Messi has ever had in games against Real Madrid, or go and watch all of the shots Erling Haaland had against Sevilla in a specific match last season. This allows us to form the kind of content that provides people with the all-important ammunition to win football debates with their friends.

The younger generations can be criticised for the way they consume media, but I think that they should be credited with how much they take in all the time, and with our output I think that the community we've built around learning is a beautiful thing. We wouldn't exist without their thirst for learning.

It's a community built around technology and analysing football in an innovative way, but there's a level of respect here between the people who interact with my output. We want to create a community that looks after its members, that cares about the players on the pitch as actual people, that cares about football itself. There's enough anger elsewhere, so we want this to be a space for people to communicate with each other before a game, during a game or after a game, wherever they are in the world.

Most of my audience come from the same place as me: they are sat in a bedroom on their own watching football.

Statman Dave was interviewed by James Bird

A View from the Pitch

Peter Harvey, aged 9, with the FA Cup, 1939
Julian Germain, 1991

Spectacle

The world's longest-running football tournament, the Football Association Cup, was created in 1871 as a way to build excitement and support for the newly developing sport. The first FA Cup final took place at the Oval cricket ground in London, drawing a crowd of 2,000 people. The winner's trophy is one of the most coveted in English football.

LEFT

FA Cup, 1900

RIGHT

The winning design for the FA Cup made by Fattorini & Sons in 1911

THE ORIGINAL DESIGN FOR
THE ENGLISH FOOTBALL ASSOCIATION CUP.

The FA Cup pictured in the London silver workshops of luxury brand Thomas Lyte, official silverware supplier to the FA. In 2014, they were commissioned to recreate the treasured Cup, having restored the previous edition for eighteen years.

Football

Steph Houghton of Manchester City
Women kisses the Women's FA Cup
trophy. SSE Women's FA Cup final,
Manchester City v. West Ham, Wembley
Stadium, 4 May 2019

An independent Women's Football
Association was formed in 1969,
shortly before the FA's ban on women
playing was finally lifted in England.
A year later it introduced its own Cup
tournament, in which seventy-one teams
from across England, Scotland and
Wales participated. The current trophy,
commissioned in 1997, incorporates
three lionesses, two of which form the
handles of the cup.

Spectacle

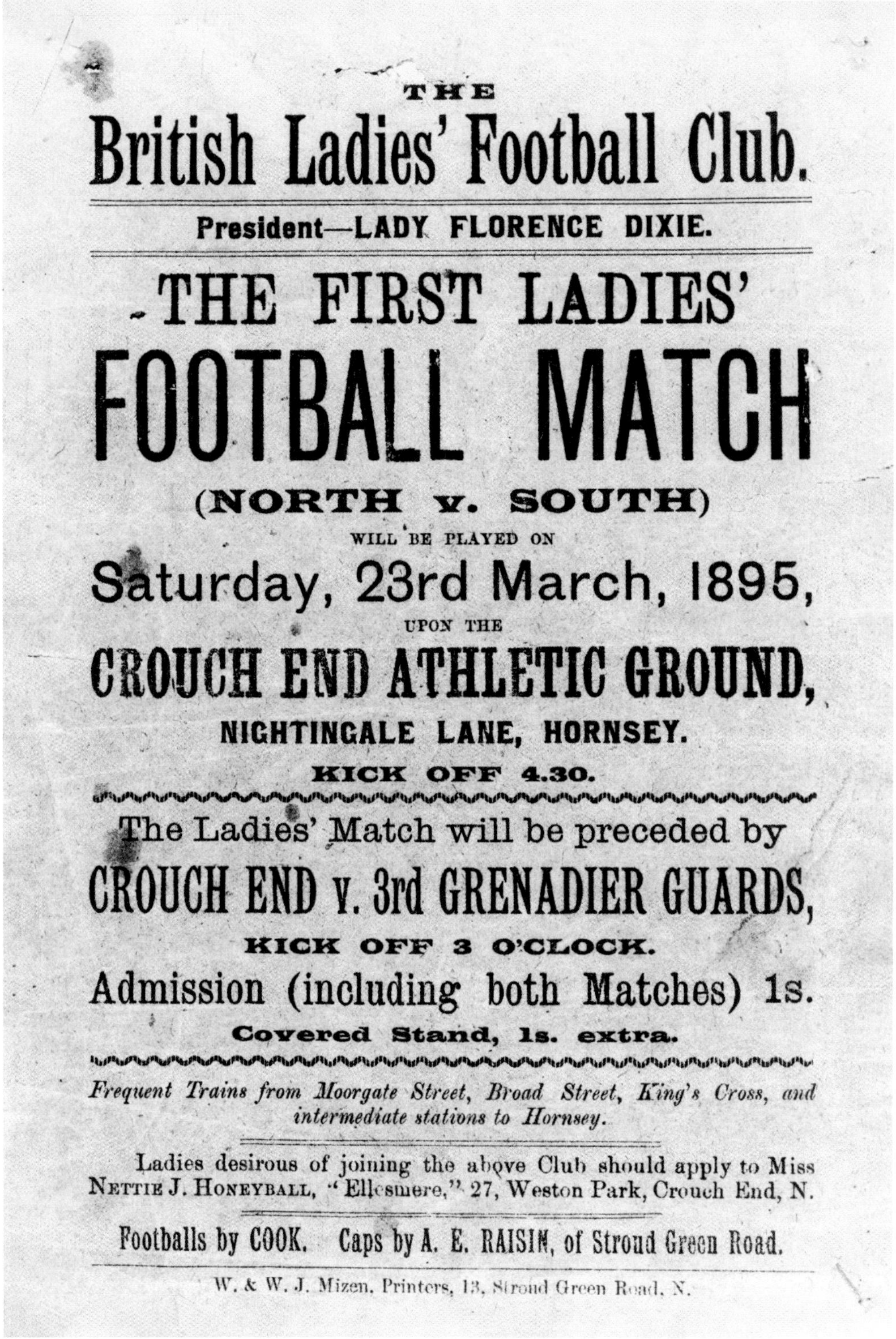

Advertisement for a women's football match, 1895

MISS NETTIE HONEYBALL, CAPTAIN OF THE BRITISH LADIES' FOOTBALL CLUB,
IN HER FOOTBALL COSTUME.
FROM A PHOTOGRAPH BY MESSRS. RUSSELL AND SONS, BAKER STREET, W.

Nettie Honeyball, founder of the British
Ladies' Football Club – the first women's
football team – in 1895

Nine house caps Rugby School, c.1850s

The British tradition of awarding
caps to players originated at
Rugby School, an elite English boys'
school where pupils played Rugby
football. Velvet caps were awarded to
leading players and worn for official
photographs. Differences in colour and
design distinguished which House the
players belonged to.

SFC schoolboy's cap, 1901

Awarding caps was introduced into football in 1886 as a means of incentivising players and providing a sense of reward. Initially, international tournaments were played only between the home nations of Great Britain, with the colour of the cap changing depending on England's opponents: purple for Scotland, red for Wales and white for Ireland (a united country at that time).

Sheila Parker's Women's Football Association cap against France, 1970s

In what was an act of gender discrimination, the FA initially refused to supply caps to female players, so theirs had to be handmade, often by the players themselves. Sheila Parker was appointed as first captain of the England women's team in 1972 and remained so until 1976.

Spectacle

The idea of a global competition for professional footballers came from former FIFA President Jules Rimet. The original FIFA World Cup trophy, used between 1930 and 1970, was renamed in Rimet's honour in 1946. The gold-plated sterling silver and lapis lazuli cup depicted a winged figure, representing Nike, the Greek goddess of victory. It was awarded permanently in 1970 to Brazil, the first nation to win three times, so a second trophy was commissioned which has been used from 1974 to the present.

Winner's replica of the Jules Rimet trophy, 1970

Football

FIFA World Cup™ final, Wembley
Stadium, London, 30 July 1966: England
4–2 West Germany

Spectacle

FIFA World Cup™ final, Estadio Monumental, Buenos Aires, 25 June 1978: Argentina 3–1 Netherlands

A major design element of the World Cup tournament is the poster, whose style and motifs capture and communicate something of the host nation's identity and aspirations. The first FIFA World Cup took place in 1930 in Uruguay, with thirteen participating countries. An official FIFA Women's World Cup has been running since 1991, although unofficial world championships date back to 1970. In the words of Uruguayan journalist and novelist Eduardo Galeano, the tournament has the power to 'pull tiny countries out of the shadows of universal anonymity'. Often taking on an iconic status, many FIFA World Cup posters have been designed by renowned artists and graphic designers.

OPPOSITE

1970 FIFA World Cup™ Official Poster

Football

Football

OPPOSITE CLOCKWISE FROM TOP LEFT

FIFA World Cup™ Official
Posters; 1954, 1962, 1938, 1966

RIGHT

Official Poster for the first
FIFA World Cup™ in 1930

Spectacle

XI
Campeonato
Mundial
de Fútbol

Junio 1978

Buenos Aires
Córdoba
Mar del Plata
Mendoza
Rosario

Argentina '78

Football

Spectacle

Football

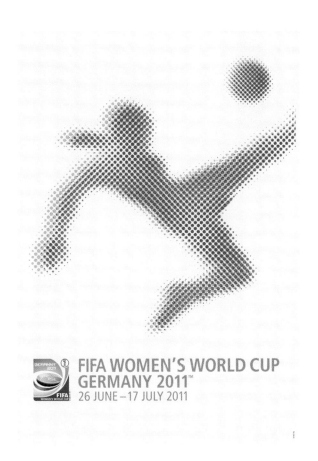

Nick Barnes' Sunderland AFC match day
books, BBC Radio Newcastle

Football commentator Nick Barnes covers
Sunderland's matches for BBC Radio
Newcastle. For each match, he creates
a detailed colour-coded two-page
spread, covering background information
on the opposition team, and updates of
the action in real-time.

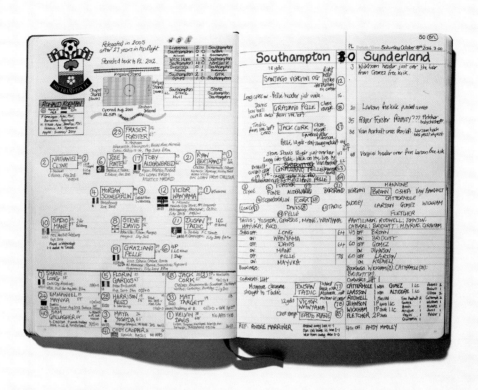

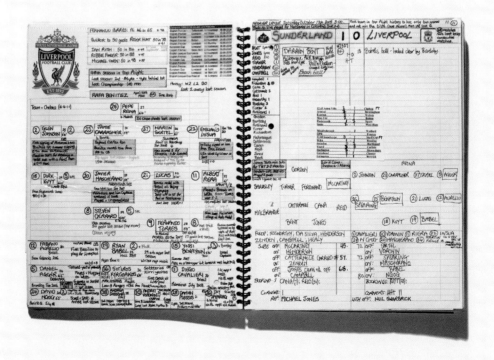

A minute-by-minute illustrated guide
to the 2019 FIFA Women's World Cup™
Minute Books, commissioned by It's Nice That
Illustrations by Charlotte Ager,
Laylah Amarchih, Laurie Avon, Hannah
Buckman, Sebastian Curi, Jiye Kim,
Rebeka Lukošus, Luis Mazón, Sean O'Brien,
Haley Tippman, Amber Vittoria and Gracey
Zhang, 2019

Minute Books is a performative press that
uses illustration and design to present
real-time responses to live events.
The illustrations created during the event
are scanned, processed and compiled
into a book. Here twelve illustrators
captured every game from the 2019
FIFA Women's World Cup. The semi-final,
in which England played the United
States, attracted a television audience
of 11.7 million, making it the most-watched
programme in the UK at that time.

Siegerflieger, Juergen Teller, 2014

One of several projects dedicated to
football by German photographer and
football fan Juergen Teller, this series
documents the photographer, his family
and students through 2014, a year
when Germany won the FIFA World Cup.
Siegerflieger literally translates as 'the
victor's plane', the affectionate name
given to the German team's customised
aircraft. The images capture the deep and
intense emotional investment unique to
football fandom. The anguish, euphoria
and even humour of watching a match on
television is universal. It has become a
way to connect loved ones and strangers,
and to reinforce national identity.

Spectacle

5

Play

Football Manager: Life Imitating Art Imitating Life Imitating Art
Miles Jacobson

When Miles Jacobson first played the game now known as *Football Manager* in 1992, it didn't even feature the names of real players. The intricacies and economics of licensing meant that the players had fake names, the interface design was essentially an Excel spreadsheet, and you couldn't watch the matches that the team you'd poured your heart and knowledge into were involved in. But he was hooked. The game that Paul and Oliver Collyer had created from their bedroom was unlike anything that had gone before, or anything that would come after. For the first time, you, the user, were in control of a football club, making decisions that impacted games, attendances, finances. It was designed, as Miles says, in a way that made it a 'living and breathing world'.

Football Manager involves a user choosing from over 2,500 clubs from around the world, and then making informed decisions to lead that club to glory. To those who don't play, it can still look like a collection of football-related spreadsheets. But every single element of the game – from transfers, to manager–fan relations, to scouting techniques – is designed to represent real life, and for the user to make real-life decisions based on these attributes and their outcomes. These in-game decisions range from deciding whether to act on an extraordinarily detailed player transfer suggestion from an in-game scout that you have decided to employ on a continent 5,000 kilometres away because of a specific attribute you require to make your in-game team truly your team, to whether the manager avatar designed to represent you should have a moustache or not. The average *Football Manager* player in 2021 racked up over 369 hours of playing time.

That living and breathing world has made its way to its thirtieth anniversary, and year on year, everything about it gets bigger – more players, more stats, more clubs, more detailed animations to watch your team's matches – and because of this, the line between 'real' and *Football Manager* has blurred to the point where players' real-life careers can be shaped by someone identifying them in a *Football Manager* game, and basing a real-life decision on their in-game attributes. Some footballers, such as Stoke-on-Trent-born and now Chile international Ben Brereton, have even made their national team debuts because of keen-eyed gamers finding out their family tree via the game. People are obsessed, with real-life holidays, relationships, jobs and the team a user supports all impacted by what happens in the game.

Sports Interactive is now the world's leading developer of football management simulations, and its director Miles Jacobson, who joined the company when it was little more than a bedroom project in 1994, has seen every aspect of its evolution.

●

The very first football management games tended to reset at the end of every season a user played. All of your progress was gone, players weren't real, stats were randomised. You felt that while you were in control of *your* team, everything else was being done by a dice roll. What Paul and Oliver had designed from their bedroom using spreadsheets and numbers changed all of that. It was a game where not only you were making decisions, but the game was too. Nothing was random, everything followed rules, and the chunks of the game that you weren't controlling made as much sense as those that you were.

They had created a suspension of disbelief, and that is still a central pillar to the studio today.

The very first version of the game was completely text-based, with no 3D or even 2D match engine to let you watch your team play. It used words, and forced you to use your imagination with what was happening on the pitch. It was essentially a pretty ugly spreadsheet containing more numbers, and therefore more data, than any football games previously. But it was designed in a way that had to be easy to read.

When someone joins the studio now, one of the things they see as part of their induction pack is a video, and part of that is about what you would call 'canon' in the film world. The Marvel and *Star Wars* universes do this incredibly well, where lots of films feature hundreds or even thousands of characters, and they all have to fit into a storyline that makes sense.

The *Football Manager* canon is now at around 400,000 people from the real football world drawn from 116 divisions in 51 countries. That living, breathing world is the basis of everything we do.

And whenever anyone in the studio is designing anything, they have to be thinking about what fits into the game's world so that the jigsaw puzzle pieces fit together seamlessly. For it to all seem realistic, every person you interact with in the game needs to feel real, and that's what allows people to escape from their world into a dream football one. In a real world where so many people work in jobs they have to do to live, we want to create a separate world that allows them to play.

●

The game itself is created not just by us, but by the community, and at any one time we have a database of around 5,000 to 6,000 suggestions of features to add to the game. These could come from online forums dedicated to the game, they could come directly from somebody in our team, they could come from real-life professional training sessions that I attend, or from people who work in football – managers, assistant managers, players, directors. We call it the bookshelf.

These features range from redesigning where a button on the interface sits, to adding a whole new feature that reinterprets how you manage your own team and therefore narrative, such as the Data Hub. You could argue that we've played a role in making data analysis a bigger part of the real footballing landscape and, beginning with *FM21*, we wanted to go even further and revolutionise the depth of data and analysis available within *Football Manager*. We wanted to give users the power to harness the same detailed metrics and reporting methods that top teams use to find a winning edge over their rivals. Using the 'Ask For' system, users can explore even more detailed reports from their in-game analysts on a wide variety of data in just the same way that real-life managers study analysis to inform their pre-match planning, test their assumptions and strategise for success. This could be scatter graphs on shot data, tables on expected goals (xG) or bar graphs on Match Momentum to give you a clear perception of the flow of a match so you can see where the momentum shifted over the course of ninety minutes.

The Data Hub not only allows you to access more information at a faster rate, but you're also more in control than ever before over what insights you receive from your analysts.

●

Each player has around 200 individual attributes that define how they are going to play. You see some of those on screen – physical, technical and mental attributes – and then there are some hidden ones. And all these numbers feed directly into algorithms that create an output, or decision, that the player will make on the pitch.

Examples of the 3D Match Engines used in the *Football Manager* series

We're simulating everything. Every footballer on the pitch and everyone on the bench – all the substitutes and the coaches – are making decisions every quarter of a second, unless the ball is near the goal mouth, in which case they can be making decisions every eighth of a second.

With every decision the player has to make, they will have a decision-making tree surrounding them, of all the different things that they could do at that point. Their attributes feed into the percentage chance of them making that decision, and then they will make a decision based on those percentage chances.

If, in the decision tree, a defender has the choice, are they going to tackle? If they can attack, are they going to stay on their feet or are they going to go down? Are they going to back off? Are they going to press you and then instigate another chance for the attacker to make?

Even if something only has a two per cent chance of happening, that might still be the decision: it's just got a much smaller chance of being made than something that has a ninety per cent chance. What the players aren't doing is working out whether it's the right decision or not; they're working out whether it's the decision they would make – even if that's not the decision you want them, or expect them, to make. It's why players miss open goals.

In every game that is played on *Football Manager*, around 450,000 decisions are made per match.

●

In 2002, then Crystal Palace assistant manager Ray Houghton was the first person from within football to take up a role in deciding on designs within the game. By this time, our database and scouting team were very accomplished, and he called me to say 'I need a left back.' That's a real-life player for his real-life team. He didn't have email, so I faxed him over a list and we got to know each other quite well. After he'd left Crystal Palace, I asked if he wanted to come and work with us as a consultant. Ray's job was to watch our match engine and to tell us when he thought players were out of position. I remember him watching throw-ins, and he would say, 'That guy should be over there', and I would

ask, 'What, you mean two pixels that way?' He didn't know what a pixel was, but he knew where players would be, so we'd adjust the design of our match engine accordingly.

The first time we found out that we'd crossed over the bridge from being a video game to being part of real-life football was when André Villas-Boas was chief scout at Chelsea under José Mourinho. He was asked in a newspaper interview about how he was finding all these brilliant young players that nobody had heard of before, and answered that it was through the game. There were still only around twelve of us making the game at that point, whereas now there are 230 of us.

There's also the famous anecdote of then Rangers manager Alex McLeish being told by his fourteen-year-old son that he should sign a young Argentinian player who looked good in Barcelona's youth team on the game. They actually tried to. His name was Lionel Messi.

Clubs now use our data, whether they're buying it from us or not, to make decisions about who to buy. Agents call me up, managers speak to me, players call to say that their attributes aren't quite right. The line between the designed game, and the real-life game, is now more blurred than ever before.

●

We've been working on women's football for some time now. A few people inside football are aware of this, as we've been talking to them about it behind the scenes, but signing Tina Keech-Henderson as our Head of Women's Football Research was the catalyst for the announcement in November 2020 that we were adding the women's game to *FM*. Tina was having to go and get people to sign non-disclosure agreements to even be able to talk to them, so we had to announce it properly.

Our existing database has taken thirty years to build and design, and there's a lot of information that we need to research in terms of adding a new team, let alone multiple leagues.

To get our women's database right we will have to examine every single in-game attribute and define exactly how we judge the data; attributes such as pace, acceleration and agility will likely stay with the same range, but some attributes may need a different scale. These figures also feed into our match engine of course, and work done in this area (for example, looking at the height of players and how that may affect how they play) will be of benefit for the match engine overall.

And data is just one of many elements that are going to need careful consideration.

Women's body shapes are different from men's and so is their bone structure, so we have no choice but to go back to the beginning and recreate all of our existing motion-captured animation data using female players.

Then there are other questions we have to ask ourselves, such as how detailed should we go initially? There is a lot of existing literature available about the impact of the menstrual cycle on training and injuries, but how do we incorporate this without it having a major effect on gameplay? And what about pregnancy? If we have pregnant players and staff in-game, do we need different 3D models for the different stages?

This leaves us with more than 100,000 strings to rewrite … and then translate into nineteen languages. This works out to be approximately 3,000,000 words, which is more than the Bible. This is a simpler task for some languages than it is for others; Danish, for example, has no adjectival agreement or other gender-specific grammar considerations, so we should in theory be able to batch-translate 'he' to 'she' (for example). With many other languages (including French and German) that's simply not possible and each string will have to be retranslated from scratch.

Our design team is about to start work on taking the information we've gathered to date and turning that into specific tasks and a full design document. As with most of *FM*'s features, that document will give us a multi-year roadmap for engineering tasks. Nothing in *FM* is ever finished – there is always more we can add – and the same will be the case with women's football.

It won't be a case of just adding it, but it will continue to grow along with the rest of the world that we create for you to manage in.

Miles Jacobson was interviewed by James Bird

The E-Sports Boom
Russell Jones

In 2020, the year that Premier League revenue fell for the first season due to the pandemic and reduced crowds in grounds, the e-sports economy saw a year-on-year growth of around 15.7 per cent. Playing games online has very quickly evolved from being an escape from reality that allows people to play out their dreams and nightmares via a digital medium, to a place of genuine community and legitimate income, and an arena to provide entertainment to vast audiences. Crowds watching live football matches inside stadiums can now be outstripped by the number of people watching games of EA Sports' *FIFA*, and Wolverhampton Wanderers' General Manager of Marketing and Growth, Russell Jones, is at the forefront of innovative thinkers making the e-sports pillar an important part of the club. As one of the twelve original English football league members from 1888, Wolves has a long, distinguished history that scales the peaks of victory and the depths of defeat. With a recent change in ownership looking to take the club to new heights, here Russell explains why the world of e-sports is one that can't be ignored.

●

When people talk about 'brand' with regard to football clubs, some fans can be quite offended, and that has to be understood in the context of the history of the game. But it's a part of the game that is crucial to being able to perform on the pitch.

At Wolves, we see the brand sitting at the top of the tree, and under that sit a number of pillars. One of those pillars is the football club, and that will always be the team, the crucial part of the community, and it is about delivering emotional experiences to amazing fans.

E-sports is another of those pillars, and we see that as a completely standalone pillar with its own fan base. And that's important.

With a game like *FIFA*, there is an easier correlation and synergy between the football club and the e-sports pillar, but with games that aren't associated with football like *League of Legends* and *Rocket League*, there's no immediately clear mutual association, and so fans of clubs who want to keep the club 'pure' might not necessarily understand that straightaway. But this e-sports pillar is being

Wolves fans make their way to watch a football match at Molineux, their stadium in central Wolverhampton, 1959

built alongside the club, aiming to acquire new fans through a different profile. So it can be difficult to communicate.

With something like *FIFA*, a game that involves a user taking control of individual players in a 3D match engine, it's easier to tell that story. There are our staff and teams within the club trying to sign players for the actual pitch at all times, but there is another team working really hard on scouting out another set of players for e-sports. One of our *FIFA* gamers is a young Brazilian called Flavio.

Flavio is a twenty-one-year-old who supports his whole family through his career in e-sports. In 2018, I remember sitting in Molineux Stadium watching Wolves playing Aston Villa. At the same time, I was streaming the FUT Champions Cup in Bucharest on my mobile, and Flavio, or FIFILZA, was competing against Tekkz. There were 31,000 people in the stadium at the Wolves match, and over 100,000 people watching the livestream. I regularly tune in to Wolves Esports *QQ Speed* or *Honor of Kings* games in China where over one million fans will be joining the stream. The HoK team is the jewel in crown, with our acquisition in September 2021 a multi-million-dollar investment. For Wolves Esports, we have five competitive teams in China with more than eighteen million social media followers: more than twice the social follows of the Football Club. This exposure brings new fans

The E-Sports Boom

Wolverhampton Wanderers 2021–2 team photo

to the brand and new commercial opportunities to the club. It's worth understanding that there are nearly three billion gamers across the world. It's a huge opportunity for football clubs. We want to be a player in this market, so that people will follow Wolves online, and feel engaged with our football club.

This convergence provides extraordinary engagement and growth opportunities to progressive football clubs. The recent lockdown, for example, saw people of all generations take to gaming as a way to communicate with their friends. Football clubs will ultimately compete with gaming and e-sports for attention, so rather than fight your competitor, we took the view that we should embrace the industry in order for us to learn and grow.

There are a number of facets that go beyond the numbers, for football clubs. At Wolves, one of those is the development of e-sports in the community. We're working really hard with the University of Wolverhampton on academies, including looking at building them in Brazil and China to develop the next e-sports champions, and also looking at live experiences. We're working with the local university to develop a venue to host not only academy events, but host e-sports events. This means that the city can go on the map as an e-sports venue.

A strong visual identity is crucial for success: everything has to link back to the club and the shirt. Wolves are very lucky to have a predator as a visual and brand reference. We are also lucky to have such striking and rich historic colours, with our gold and black. These are a gift for this sector in terms of differentiating us from other clubs, so it's imperative for us to use them to make us more visually appealing than our competitors. During the height of the pandemic in 2020, we

Wolves e-sports team graphics

launched branded 'skins' – a type of cosmetic outfit gamers may equip their gaming avatar with and use in-play – in the *Fortnite* game franchise, which provided us with an opportunity to reach and engage with thirty million daily active players. It was crucial that our skin was 'cool', visually different from our football jersey and aesthetically exciting. We also have digital product available to the players of the *NBA2k22* game - the only football club to have this presence.

The challenge visually is to create something that will appeal across a wide range of demographics but remains sympathetic to your overall brand style. Our brand narrative is 'the ultimate challenger club', meaning that we are outside what is now considered the traditional 'top six' of the Premier League but are finding innovative ways to break their dominance. We don't set brand guidelines and stick with them for the rest of eternity. Instead we set some parameters but accept that our brand style will continually adapt and evolve.

Being brave and progressive is a fundamental part of our DNA.

Russell Jones was interviewed by James Bird

On Playing the Game
Percy M. Young

Percy M. Young (1912–2004) was best known in his lifetime as a musicologist – he wrote dozens of biographies of classical composers, with a particular passion for Elgar; he also wrote books for children, and music of his own, as well as working for many years as director of music at Wolverhampton College of Technology. But his other lifelong passion was football: he published books charting the fortunes of Manchester United and his own club, Wolverhampton Wanderers, along with the first ever history of the British game in general. *Football Facts and Fancies* (1950), from which this excerpt is taken, is a lively collection of football trivia and thoughtful reflections on the art of spectatorship. In many ways it captures a vanished era.

●

Football, whether for performers or spectators, renews childhood. Instinctively we return to what we were. We are serious about trivialities.

It is a great thing to be able to take seriously what is unimportant. When we can do this, we can begin to take seriously what is important.

Those who condemn us watchers I hate. They have neither wit nor imagination. They have forgotten all that is worth remembering and would deprive us too of our dreams. 'The Puritan hated bear-baiting,' wrote Lord Macaulay, 'not because it gave pain to the bear, but because it gave pleasure to the spectator.' And so with some modern Puritans who would have us away from our pastime on Saturday afternoons. (For bears, however, read Wolves.)

It is part of my argument, if what I say can be considered an argument, that the regular weekly million are dreamers. Dreamers are often poets. What a poet says is frequently more important than what a man who is not a poet says. It is imaginatively truthful.

We spend most of our adult lives in avoiding the truth. We are polite, discreet, ready to compromise. We hate to appear odd, not realising that by avoiding eccentricity we acquire it. On Saturday afternoons we find ourselves. We speak the truth (at any rate as it appears to us), we appreciate art ('beautiful' is allowed

Spectators packed into The Den – even on the floodlights and scoreboard – for a Millwall v. Newcastle United FA Cup match, 1957

to most of us on that day only), we love our neighbour (or – paradoxically what is the same thing – hate him) without qualification.

All because once we did, in our own way, what those we watch do, in theirs. We, in fact, like to think that we know how.

As for me I will watch football anywhere. There is a game going on as I write. The children are at it. Boys and girls, all under six, over the flower beds, among the cabbages. Rules do not exist. Fouls are frequent, injuries sometimes – but briefly – insupportable. The natural end of the game is dinnertime, a broken window, a refusal to put the ball down. There is no end to the game. Neither is there, to be truthful, when Manchester City play Manchester United. Each meeting is an episode. At the end of all time that contest may be determined, but not before.

Extract from *Football: Facts and Fancies* (1950).
Reprinted by permission of the Cadbury Research Library, University of Birmingham.

On Playing the Game

A View from the Pitch:

The Whole World on Your Table
Gareth Christie

Subbuteo has been inspiring heartbreak and ecstasy via plastic and felt for over seventy years, and Gareth Christie has been at the centre of the game's community since he was a kid. Gareth was twelve years old in 1989 when he walked into his friend Greg's house and his life changed forever.

On a green felt pitch inside his house, Greg was flicking about some plastic figurines painted to wear Dundee United kits, the team Gareth supported. Transfixed by how the players glided around the pitch on their bases and knocked the ball to each other towards a goal with a net made of string, he was hooked. And just two years later, Gareth was crowned Scottish Junior Subbuteo Champion. Now Gareth is a designer and maker at FlicksForKicks, a company he founded with his dad that creates incredibly beautiful and detailed custom Subbuteo tables.

●

I left school to become an architectural technician apprentice, and did that for six years before going to study Computer Arts. I'd gear all of my projects towards my interests, and my final-year project involved creating a digital learning tool for Subbuteo. The rules have always been pretty vague, and I wanted to simplify that using technology, but really I wanted to get people to play the game face to face and keep the community going as interest waned.

A FlicksForKicks Subbuteo table

Subbuteo is exciting because it's a fully immersive replica of football. There's something for every fan, whether you're into playing matches with friends, running your own solo leagues, model-making to build a stadium or painting your favourite kits. With a history going back to 1947, it's also wrapped up in nostalgia, touching the hearts of so many of us, as we tried to emulate our favourite teams or players as kids growing up. The design of the distinctive green packaging through each era, the catalogues with floodlights, the memories of the terracing and pitch-side accessories you'd dream about are all conjured up by those little plastic men. And like football for many, it's an escape from the pressures of modern life. Subbuteo transports you back to arguably simpler times.

We're a father and son family business, and everything is handmade. My dad is multi-talented with traditional practical skills; great with his hands. He handles the woodworking and painting side for tables, metalworking for the goals, and we problem-solve on design together.

I'm trained in digital art and design, and also love to get into the details of the craft aspect, so I sketch design concepts, produce graphics, 3D print prototypes, and do the hands-on intricate finishing work on the tables.

The personalised table design process starts with information gathering and listening, which helps us to walk in the customer's shoes. When people share their stories and happy memories, they're telling us what's important to them, so we use this for inspiration in the build. Personalised graphics might be a dedication to a loved one, a hook to remember an iconic football moment, songs from the terraces. This all feeds into deciding on what we're making, the design details, and especially where gifts are concerned, how we could delight someone through an emotional connection.

Subbuteo is about manual dexterity; it's an analogue skill. Video games are designed to have a learning curve, but with Subbuteo it's more difficult. There's the manual technique and all the rules. It can feel a bit daunting at first, because there's no step by step. Then you have to react to the other player's playing style and the situation of the game as well. When you play in competitions, nerves become a part of this. You can get shaky hands, and you really have to control your emotions.

When I was younger it was all about winning and trophies, but later on in life it's about friendships and meeting up with people. You can go pretty much anywhere in the world and have this common game you can chat about, with everyone really welcoming you wherever you go.

Gareth Christie was interviewed by James Bird

A View from the Pitch

A View from the Pitch:

A Whole New Lens
Matthew Barrett

Goal Click is a global storytelling organisation that aims to help people understand one another and the world through football. Co-founded in 2014 by Matthew Barrett, the initiative is very simple: Goal Click sends analogue cameras to people connected to football and asks them to take pictures of what they do and see around them. From telling stories in South Sudan through a partnership with the UN Refugee Agency, to collaborations with New York City FC, exploring the grassroots scene in the Big Apple, Goal Click shows the game at its best, most democratic, most playful and most impactful. Here is Matthew on why that's so important.

●

At Goal Click, every piece of content is from a first-person perspective. This isn't about outsiders coming into someone's life or a community and telling stories about them. It's about giving people the power, freedom and control to tell their own story as they see it. We're active in about 150 different countries with all backgrounds: from amputee and disability football in Sierra Leone to refugee camps in Jordan to community projects to fan culture and the elite game. Our aim is to tell the story of the whole world through the lens of football, and to provide room for the stories of the underdogs, the silenced, the marginalised.

The 2019 FIFA Women's World Cup saw the women's game finally get some of the exposure it deserves. We've always covered both the men's and women's game equally, and ahead of the tournament we set out with the intention of telling women's stories from both a grassroots level and also the professional internationals on the pitch. For instance, we had Beth Mead and Lucy Bronze involved from the England team, Sam Mewis and Kelley O'Hara from the US, Lauren Silver from Jamaica and Miranda Nild from Thailand. We were blown away with the enthusiasm from the teams, clubs and federations, and launched the series with the *New York Times* while holding exhibitions in Lyon and Paris with COPA90. The photos that came back were very special in many ways.

We got very intimate, behind-the-scenes insights. Could an outsider have taken the photo that Sam Mewis took of Rose Lavelle and Alex Morgan recovering in an ice bath at

FC Nordsjælland (FCN) women's team celebrate winning the Cup Final in 2019

the US Women's National Team camp in San Jose? No, I don't think they could. The brief for a Goal Click storyteller is always to capture their football life and their felt community from their own perspective.

We use analogue cameras for three reasons. Equality: it's important to us that a player from the US has the same tool as a young girl from the mountains of Peru. The second is intentionality. We take hundreds of photos on our smartphones and maybe never look at them again. Having just one roll with twenty-seven photos means Goal Click storytellers have to be more intentional and patient with what they choose to capture. It puts value on a single photo. The third is that using analogue cameras means that the images are unique, imperfect and capture a specific moment.

There's the culture of playfulness: no fabrication, no posing, the feeling of ease, no pressure of someone telling you what to do. But it can expose the darker side, too. The lack of resources, the obstacles that are in the way — even for elite footballers, especially at the Women's World Cup where wealthier nations have so much more funding and experience.

I want people who look at the photos to be curious about what's going on in the wider context. What is happening in Brazil? North Korea? London? What is happening with seventy-year-old American women playing football? I want people to feel challenged by it. A viewer might have fixed views on gender, around refugees, about specific countries like Russia, and with Goal Click, I want them to feel challenged when they see a different perspective.

Matthew Barrett was interviewed by James Bird

A View from the Pitch

Villa Hayes, Paraguay

Posts, Neville Gabie, 1996–present

Posts is an ongoing body of work developed by South African artist Neville Gabie over the last twenty-five years. A series of football photographs devoid of action, it is intended as a reflection on the universality of our desire to play, no matter where. Gabie has said of the project, 'with minimal means these goalposts ... encapsulate our dreams and fantasies, and the uniqueness of "place", in the language which is universally understood.'

Football

TOP
Dunkirk, France

MIDDLE
Khorixas, Namibia

BOTTOM
Skopje, North Macedonia

OVERLEAF
Massel Bel Abbes, Tunisia

Play

Baines cards, John Baines
1885–1920

Collectable sports cards, known as Baines cards, became popular in the 1890s in northern England, contributing to the flourishing of a collecting and trading culture that continues today. Bradford toy retailer John Baines was one of the earliest producers of these cards, which were printed in the thousands. Notable sportsmen were depicted on the front and advertisements on the back, with cards covering both professional and amateur sports clubs.

Football

Play

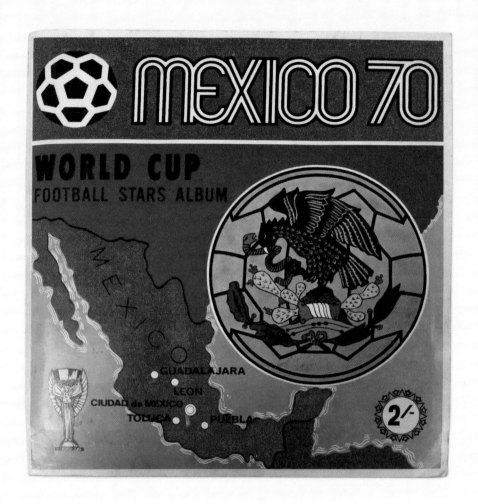

Panini sticker album, Mexico, 1970

The Panini sticker factory in São Paulo
during the FIFA World Cup™, Brazil 2014
Tom Jenkins for *The Guardian*

Italian company Panini began
producing football stickers in 1961
with the release of a collection based
on the top domestic league, Serie A.
They published their first FIFA
World Cup trading cards and sticker
album for the 1970 FIFA World Cup
in Mexico. The stickers were an instant
hit with children, initiating a craze
for collecting and trading them.

Football

Play

STERREN-ALBUM **VOETBALSTERREN**

NEDERLANDSE EREDIVISIE
1968-1969

1.50

266

Football

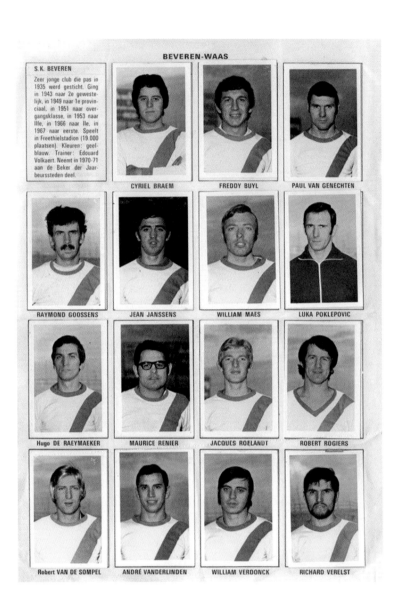

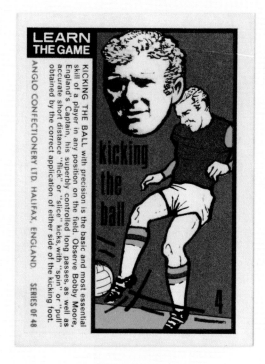

Bubble gum cards, 1969

OPPOSITE

Fan scrapbook, Arsenal, 1971

This fan-made scrapbook features
photographs and press cuttings
relating to the maker's favourite club.
In contrast to official publications,
such as football annuals, it is a highly
personal compilation that illustrates the
particular interests of an individual fan.

Football

Oldest table football game, made in
Preston, 1884

Football

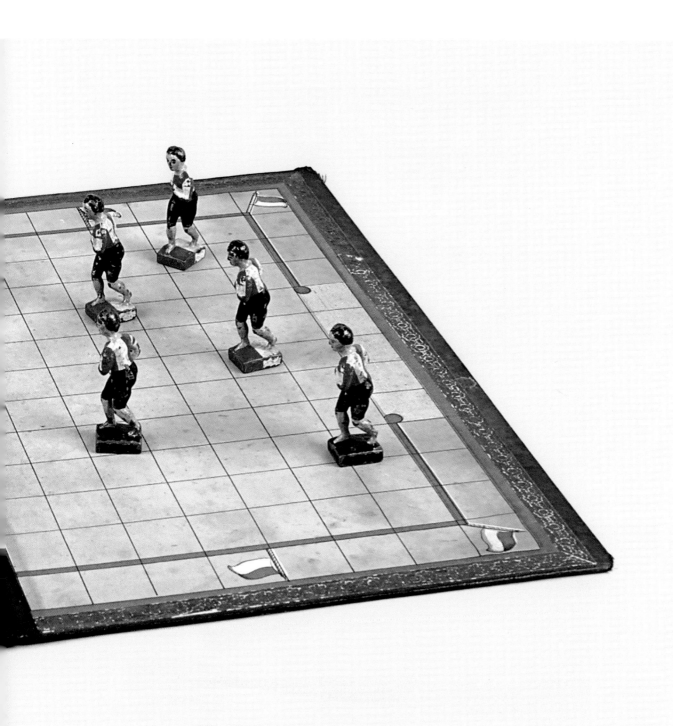

Play

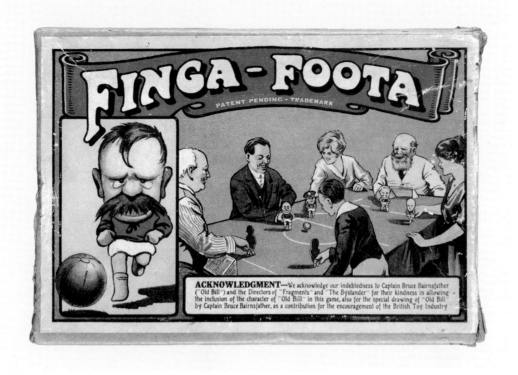

Football

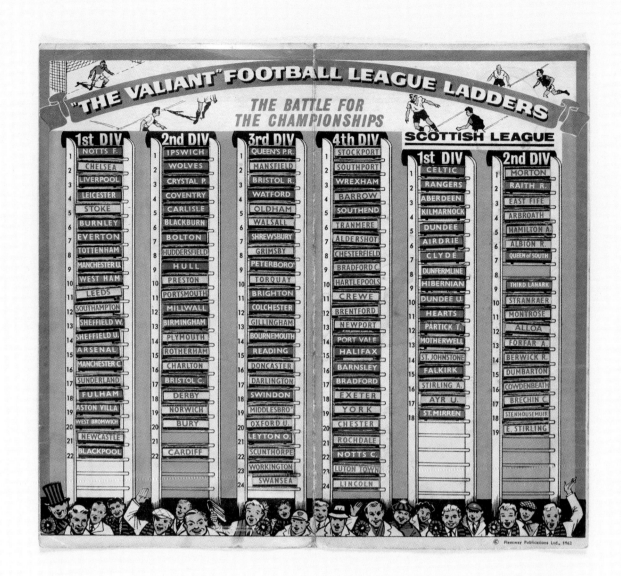

'The Valiant' Football League Ladders, 1962

Matchbox football game, Japan, 1930s

Football

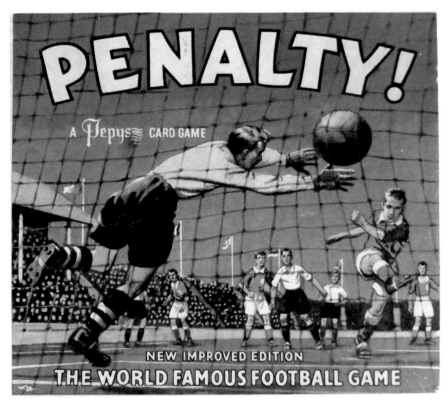

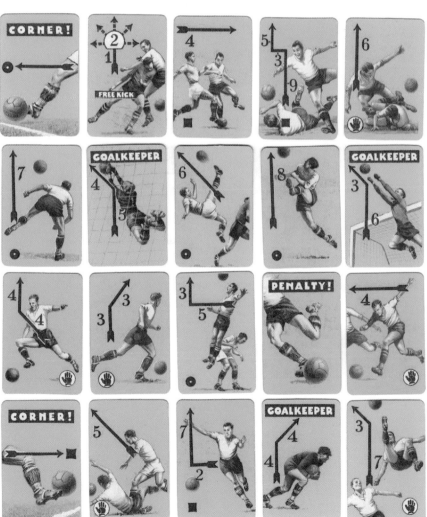

Play

Men playing blow football, 1950s

Blow football is a tabletop game where the objective is to blow a small, lightweight ball into the opponent's goal. The game is often played with whatever materials are at hand, such as drinking straws and ping pong balls. Boxed versions of the game, available since the 1900s, typically contained a ball, two plastic goals and enough pipes for teams of up to three players.

Football

Play

Tin of early Subbuteo figures,
Peter A. Adolph, 1949–50

Created in 1946 by Peter Adolph,
Subbuteo is a tabletop game in which
players simulate playing football by
flicking miniature players with their
fingers. Early Subbuteo sets contained
wire goal frames, a ball and cardboard
playing figures on bases made from
buttons. In 1961, Adolph introduced
the classic three-dimensional hand-
painted 'heavyweight' plastic figures.
Subbuteo offered hundreds of team kit
designs and accessories, such as special
figures for free kicks and throw-ins, TV
cameras, and even a miniature model of
Her Majesty the Queen to present the FA
Cup to the winners, as part of the game.

Football

Andrea Piccaluga, Subbuteo World
Junior Champion in 1979

Play

'Subbuteo Superheroes' series, *No. 7 Left Wing. Peter Parker aka The Amazing Spiderman* and *No. 2 Full Back. Steve Rogers aka Captain America*, Julian Germain (with Nick Kidney), 1997

'Subbuteo Superheroes' is a photographic series by artist Julian Germain that captures a team of personalised Subbuteo players painted by Nick Kidney. As a shy thirteen-year-old, Kidney transformed the figures into his favourite comic book superheroes, sharing them with Germain as an adult. Germain's images are reminiscent of the football cards and stickers of his and Kidney's youth, while the scale of the prints reflects the size of the heroes in the boy's imagination.

Football

Play

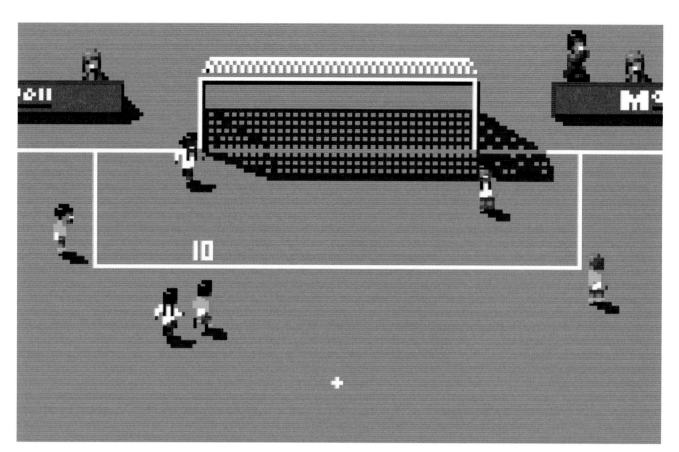

Football

Championship Manager for Atari ST
1992

Championship Manager is an early
example of the genre of football-
management simulation games. It was
first released in 1992, then rebranded
as *Football Manager* in 2005, with new
editions released annually. Players
take on the persona of a club manager,
controlling a team, developing tactics
and signing new players. The database
for the series has become one of the
most sophisticated in the gaming world.
The vast amount of data captured by
the game is now a valuable resource for
real clubs, which use it to scout players
and opposition teams.

OPPOSITE

Sensible Soccer
Jon Hare and Sensible Software
1992

Created by Jon Hare in 1992, *Sensible
Soccer* was designed to be played at
a frenetic pace and fast became a
favourite with gamers. It was the first
football game that allowed the player
to take a bird's-eye perspective on the
pitch, and offered editable national,
club and custom teams. The graphics
now have iconic status among nostalgic
games fans.

Play

First released in 1993 as *FIFA International Soccer*, FIFA is one of the most popular video games of all time. It differentiated itself from other digital games by providing a three-dimensional representation of the pitch. Updated editions, released every year, strive to simulate a real football game with increasing accuracy. Real player data is used, including rankings of skills such as passing and dribbling, with a network of more than 6,000 data reviewers deployed to ensure this information remains accurate. Female players were introduced to the FIFA series in 2015.

Football

Play

Goal Click is a project that aims to send disposable cameras around the world, encouraging people to tell stories about themselves, their communities and their country from a viewpoint relating to football. Since 2014, the project has given a multifaceted view of humanity using a diverse range of storytellers. A core principle is self-creation: Goal Click gives everyone the same tool to put their vantage point at the centre of the world.

OPPOSITE TOP

Over-seventies women's team The Sockers during the Las Vegas Friendship Cup, spring 2021. Photo: Judi Works

OPPOSITE BOTTOM

Players with RIFA (Rooklyn International Football Association), a Brooklyn-based organisation using soccer to work with refugee, asylee and immigrant youth and provide a space for connection with their peers in a safe and supportive environment. Photo: Samuel Gedeon

NEXT SPREAD

A match during the second season of the Gilgit-Baltistan Girls Football League, the first ever league for girls in the north of Pakistan. Photo: Sumaira Inayat

Play

Football

Play

Index

Illustration and caption page numbers are in *italics*.

Index

Index

Picture Credits

Every reasonable attempt has been made to identify owners of copyright. Errors and omissions notified to the publisher will be corrected in subsequent editions. Abbreviations are: T – top, B – bottom, L – left, R – right.

p. 7: H. F. Davis/Topical Press Agency/Getty Images; p. 8: PA Images/Alamy Stock Photo; p. 9: Anthony Barnett; p. 10: IMAGO/WEREK; p. 12: PA Images/Alamy Stock Photo; p. 16t: Artokoloro/Alamy Stock Photo; p.16b: Bob Thomas/Popperfoto via Getty Images/Getty Images; p.18: EMAP archive/London College of Fashion Archives; p. 19: ullstein bild/ullstein bild via Getty Images; p. 20: NIKE, Inc.; p. 23: The adidas archive/studio waldeck; p. 25: The adidas archive; p. 27: Courtesy of Gaffer. Photographer Hamish Stephenson for Nike Football; p. 29: Alan Bond (August-May); p. 30: National Football Museum; p. 31: Wayne Hutchinson/Alamy Stock Photo; p. 32: National Football Museum; p. 33: © Mirrorpix/Daily Record; p. 34: National Football Museum; p. 35: Superball; p. 36: © Co-Operative Group; pp. 37, 38, 39: PUMA Archive; p. 40: The adidas archive; p. 41: The adidas archive/studio waldeck; p. 42: PUMA Archive; p. 43, 44t: The adidas archive/studio waldeck; p. 44b: German Football Museum, Dortmund; p. 45: The adidas archive/studio waldeck; p. 46: Natural Grass; p. 47: The adidas archive/studio waldeck; pp. 48-9: NIKE, Inc.; p. 50: Kevin Blankenship/Ida Sports; p. 51: Ida Sports; p. 52, 53, 54, 55, 56-7: © Alastair Philip Wiper; p. 58: National Football Museum; p. 59t: Manchester United Museum; p. 59b: NIKE, Inc.; pp. 60, 61: National Football Museum; pp. 62, 63: Reusch; p. 64: US Patent No. 4,174,717; p. 65: Alessandro Rampazzo/AFP via Getty Images; p. 66, 67: ACME Whistles; p. 68: Fox Photos/Hulton Archive/Getty Images; p. 69: National Football Museum; p. 70t: Gerry Cranham/Offside; p. 70b: Goal Click/Brianna Visalli; p. 74t: Nomad®; p. 74b: Charlie Campbell; p. 75: Queerspace FC; pp. 76, 77: National Football Museum; p. 81: NIKE, Inc.; p. 83: Stephanie Sian Smith; p. 85: Peter Carney; p. 86: Queen's Park Football Club; p. 87: © Jon Barmby; pp. 88-9: © CSG CIC Glasgow Museums and Libraries Collection: The Mitchell Library, Special Collections; p. 90: Juventus; p. 91: ConIFA and its affiliated members; p. 92: Alex Hurst; p. 93: PA Images/Alamy Stock Photo; p. 94, 95, 96-7: National Football Museum; p. 98: The FA; p. 99: National Football Museum; p. 100: Rolls Press/Popperfoto via Getty Images/Getty Images; p. 101: Acervo Aldyr Garcia Schlee; p. 102: Umbro Ltd; p. 103: National Football Museum; p. 104-5: H. F. Davis/Topical Press Agency/Getty Images; p. 106: Phil Stephens Photography/FIFA Museum; p. 107: © FIFA Museum; p. 108: Anthony Barnett; p. 109: Paul Barnes; p. 110: Mark Leech/Offside; p. 111: Roberto Schmidt/AFP via Getty Images; p. 112: Umbro Ltd; p. 113: PA Images/Alamy Stock Photo; p. 114: James Pearson-Howes; p. 115: Fila; pp. 116, 117: Émile-Samory Fofana; pp. 118, 119, 120, 121: Ed Lazurinas/Classic Football Shirts Museum; p. 122: Jake Payne; p. 123: Peter Hooton; pp. 124-5: Gerry Cranham/Offside; pp. 126, 127t, 127bl: National Football Museum; p. 127br: Matthew Caldwell - @1_shilling; p. 128: Matthew Caldwell - @1_shilling; p. 129: National Football Museum; pp. 130, 131, 132, 133: Courtesy of Mark, Paul and Samantha Elvin; pp. 134, 135: Corbin Shaw; pp. 136, 137: Peter Carney; p. 138: © Julian Germain; p. 139: National Football Museum;

p. 140: Henry Griffin; p. 142: National Football Museum; p. 143: Peter Hooton; p. 144: National Football Museum; p. 147: Gill Sayell; p. 148: Jacqui McAssey; p. 148b: Zoe Hitchen; p. 149: Fan.Tastic Females; p. 150: Pancho Monti; p. 157: Ruedi Walti; p. 159: Clynt Garnham Sport/Alamy Stock Photo; p. 161: Pancho Monti; p. 162: National Football Museum; p. 163: © Andreas Gursky/Courtesy Sprüth Magers Berlin London/DACS 2022; p. 164t: Oleksandr Prykhodko/Alamy Stock Photo; p. 164b: Canon2260/Alamy Stock Photo; p. 166: Witters/Tim Groothuis; p. 167: Ricardo Chaves; pp. 168-9: Hulton Archive/Getty Images; p. 171: Scottish Football Museum; p. 172: British Library (Patents Department); p. 173: Gerry Cranham/Offside; pp. 174-5: H. F. Davis/Topical Press Agency/Getty Images; pp. 176, 177: © Liverpool FC & Athletic Co Ltd/LFC Museum; pp. 178, 179: Teesside Archives; pp. 180-1: Homer Sykes/Alamy Stock Photo; p. 182t: Brian Harris/Alamy Stock Photo; p. 182b: PA Images/Alamy Stock Photo; pp. 184, 185, 186: Ragazzi and Partners archive; p. 187: Riccardo Sala/Alamy Stock Photo; p. 188: © Hufton+Crow; p. 189t: © Edward Hill; p. 189b: © Tottenham Hotspur; p. 190, 191: Robert Hösl, Courtesy of Herzog & de Meuron; p. 192, 193: Herzog & de Meuron; p. 194: Render by MIR/Zaha Hadid Architects; p. 195t: Render by negativ.com/Zaha Hadid Architects; p. 195b: Zaha Hadid Architects; p. 196: © Dacian Groza; p. 197: Luís Ferreira Alves; pp. 198, 199, 200: Matteo de Mayda; p. 203: Mike Hewitt/Getty Images; p. 204: PA Images/Alamy Stock Photo; p. 209: Reuben Dangoor; p. 211: Statman Dave; p. 213: © Julian Germain; p. 214: PA Images/Alamy Stock Photo; p. 215: © With kind permission of Thomas Fattorini Ltd, Trophy and Medal Makers; p. 216: Thomas Lyte, makers of the current Emirates FA Cup trophy; p. 217: Andrew Orchard sports photography/Alamy Stock Photo; pp. 218, 219: National Football Museum; p. 220: Reproduced by kind permission of Rugby School Archives & Special Collections; p. 221, 222: National Football Museum; p. 223: Gerry Cranham/Offside; pp. 224-5: PA Images/Alamy Stock Photo; pp. 227, 228, 229, 230, 231, 232, 233: FIFA ©; p. 235: Henrik Knudsen for Eight by Eight magazine; pp. 236, 237: By Barney Fagan, Amber Vittoria, Charlotte Ager, Gracey Zhang, Hannah Buckman, Haley Tippman, Jiye Kim, Laurie Avon, Laylah Amarchih, Luis Mazón, Rebeka Lukošos, Scott Coleman, Sean O'Brien & Sebastian Curi. Commissioned by It's Nice That; pp. 239, 240: © Juergen Teller. All Rights Reserved; p. 245: Sports Interactive; p. 249: Getty Clanham/Off side; p. 250: © Wolves; p. 251: © 2021 Wolves E-Sports Club; p. 253: PA Images/Alamy Stock Photo; p. 255: © 2022 FlickForKicks Ltd. All Rights Reserved.; p. 257: Goal Click/Ásla Johannesen; pp. 258, 259, 260-1: Neville Gabie; pp. 262, 263: National Football Museum; p. 264: Berkshire Auction Rooms/Bournemouth News/Shutterstock; p. 265: Tom Jenkins; p. 266, 267: Voetbalsterren; p. 268: Anglo Confectionary Ltd; p. 269: Alan Dein; pp. 270-1, 272, 273, 274, 275: National Football Museum; pp. 276-7: TopFoto; p. 278: The Amelia, Tunbridge Wells. © Simon Kelsey/www.praxisdesign.co.uk; p. 279: Keystone Press/Alamy Stock Photo; pp. 280, 281: © Julian Germain; p. 282: Jon Hare; p. 283: Sports Interactive; p. 284, 285: © EA Sports; p. 287t: Goal Click/Judi Works; p. 287b: Goal Click/Samuel Gedeon; pp. 288-9: Goal Click/Sumaira Inayat; p. 290t: Goal Click/Abraham Bangura; p. 290b: Goal Click/YUWA/Sushanti Kumari.

Contributors and Acknowledgements

Matthew Barrett is a co-founder of Goal Click

James Bird is Creative Lead and Associate Editor at MUNDIAL

Roxanne Bottomley is a PhD candidate at Northumbria University

Nathan Buckle is a football referee in leagues across the southeast of England

Peter Carney is an artist, activist and banner maker

Gareth Christie is the owner of FlickForKicks

Reuben Dangoor is a London-based illustrator

Sam Handy is VP Design/Running at adidas

Jacques Herzog is a founding partner of Herzog & de Meuron

Iqra Ismail is Director of Women's Football at Hilltop Women's Football Club

Miles Jacobson is Studio Director at Sports Interactive

Russell Jones is General Manager for Marketing and Commercial Growth at Wolverhampton Wanderers

Trisha Lewis is the founder and manager of Romance FC

Jacqui McAssey is Senior Lecturer in Fashion Communication at Liverpool John Moores University

Justin McGuirk is Chief Curator at the Design Museum

Camila Rojas is a Boca Juniors fan from Buenos Aires

Martino Simcik Arese is Fan Culture Editor at COPA90

Statman Dave is a football analyst and tactician

Thomas Turner is a historian and author of *The Sports Shoe: A History from Field to Fashion*

Martin Tyler is a football commentator for Sky Sports

Eleanor Watson is Curator at the Design Museum

Floor Wesseling is an Amsterdam-based graphic designer

Percy M. Young was a musicologist and author of *A History of English Football* (1968)

This book was published in conjunction with the exhibition *Football: Designing the Beautiful Game* at the Design Museum, London, which opened on 8 April 2022.

Curator
Eleanor Watson

Assistant Curator
Rachel Hajek

Exhibition Project Manager
Cleo Stringer

Exhibition Coordinator
Alice Bell

Exhibition Design
OMMX

Graphic Design
Shaz Madani Studio

Content Partner
National Football Museum

Design Museum Publishing
Design Museum Enterprises Ltd
224–238 Kensington High Street
London W8 6AG
United Kingdom

designmuseum.org

First published in 2022
© 2022 Design Museum Publishing

ISBN 978 1 87200 561 4

Publishing Manager: Mark Cortes Favis
Project Editor: Robert Davies
Picture Researcher: Anabel Navarro
Assistant Editor: Rachel Hajek
Editorial Assistant: Giulia Morale
Copyeditor: Liz Dalby
Proofreader: Simon Coppock
Indexer: Nic Nicholas
Design: Shaz Madani Studio

Many colleagues at the Design Museum have
supported this book, and thanks go to them all.

Distribution

UK, Europe and select territories around the world
Thames & Hudson
181A High Holborn
London WC1V 7QX
United Kingdom
thamesandhudson.com

USA and Canada
ARTBOOK | D.A.P.
75 Broad Street, Suite 630
New York, NY 10004
United States of America
www.artbook.com

Printed in Malta by Gutenberg Press